SUMMA PUBLICATIONS, INC.

Thomas M. Hines
Publisher

William C. Carter
Editor in chief

Editorial Board

William Berg
University of Wisconsin

Germaine Brée
Wake Forest University

Michael Cartwright
McGill University

Hugh M. Davidson
University of Virginia

Elyane Dezon-Jones
Washington University

John D. Erickson
University of Kentucky

James Hamilton
University of Cincinnati

Freeman G. Henry
University of South Carolina

Norris J. Lacy
Pennsylvania State University

Jerry C. Nash
University of North Texas

Allan Pasco
University of Kansas

Albert Sonnenfeld
University of Southern California

Orders:
P.O. Box 660725
Birmingham, AL 35266-0725

Editorial Address:
2530 Mountain Brook Circle
Birmingham, AL 35223

Théophile Gautier's
España

Y aun no se van!

Théophile Gautier's
España

Kathleen Koestler

SUMMA PUBLICATIONS, INC.
Birmingham, Alabama
2002

Copyright 2002
Summa Publications, Inc.
ISBN 1-883479-37-1

Library of Congress Control Number 2002107572

Printed in the United States of America

All rights reserved.

Frontispiece illustration by Francisco de Goya, Spain, 1746-1828. *Caprichos: And Still They Don't Go!,* 18th-19th century. Etching and aquatint. ©The Cleveland Museum, 2002, Dudley P. Allen Fund, 1922.654.

*For my family
and in memory of my father
General George Robinson Mather*

Contents

Abbreviations		ix
Acknowledgments		xi
Introduction		1
Chapter I:	Gautier *poète*	5
Chapter II:	The Journey to Spain	23
Chapter III:	*España*	31
Chapter IV:	The Poems of 1840	37
Chapter V:	The Poems of 1841	45
Chapter VI:	The Poems of 1842	55
Chapter VII:	The Poems of 1843	63
Chapter VIII:	The Last Year	73
Chapter IX:	*España* Revisited	83
Notes		89
Bibliography		113
Index		119

Abbreviations

PC: *Théophile Gautier: Poésies complètes,* ed., René Jasinski, 3 vols. Paris: Nizet, 1970

BOC: *Baudelaire: Œuvres complètes,* Paris: Gallimard, Bibliothèque de la Pléiade, 1961

MM: *Mademoiselle de Maupin,* ed. A. Boschot, Paris: Garnier, 1966

VE: *Voyage en Espagne,* Paris: Charpentier, 1922

RDDM: *Revue des Deux Mondes,* Paris.

Acknowledgments

I wish above all to thank Freeman Henry for helping me shape this study. His perspective and editorial guidance have been invaluable. I am also especially grateful to Noel and Tom Kirby-Smith, whose good sense saved me from several blunders. I also want to thank Beth Adamour and Mark Smith-Soto for their encouragement. Finally, I would like to thank Constance Gosselin-Schick for her useful suggestions and Gaylor Callahan in Interlibrary Loan for always managing to find the odd book.

—*K. K.*

Introduction

*Derrière l'impassible poète d'*Emaux et Camées, *il y eut un homme qui fut blessé dans son rêve le plus cher.*
—Gabriel Brunet

THE FOLLOWING POEM, "LETRILLA," was the last composed of the forty-three poems of Théophile Gautier's *España:*

> Enfant, pourquoi tant de parure,
> Sur ton sein ces rouges colliers,
> Ta clef d'argent à ta ceinture,
> Ces beaux rubans à tes souliers?
>
> —La neige fond sur la montagne;
> L'œil bleu du printemps nous sourit.
> Je veux aller à la campagne
> Savoir si le jasmin fleurit.—
>
> Pour moi ni printemps ni campagne;
> Pour moi pas de jasmin en fleur;
> Car une peine m'accompagne,
> Car un chagrin me tient au cœur. (*PC* 2, 299)

In none of the published editions of *España* does "Letrilla" appear last, yet it is a most fitting conclusion to the volume. As the adaptation of a Spanish *copla,* it demonstrates Gautier's eventual preference for the shorter poem. As a lyric plaint, it expresses the *vox clamans* at the heart of *España,* the voice of the little-recognized poet of the mid-1840s. Gautier *poète* was of course acclaimed after the appearance of *Emaux et Camées* in 1852, and the poet of the Doyenné is now also a familiar figure. Little, however, has been written about the poetry of Gautier's middle years, notably the period that produced *España* and *Voyage en Espagne* and culminated in seven years of virtual silence. There have been book-length studies devoted to Gautier's early and mature poetry, and P. E. Tennant's and Constance Gosselin-Schick's studies are recent attempts to place the whole corpus of Gautier's poetic achievement in perspective. But the poet of the 1840s—the poet of *España*—remains largely unknown. This small volume has generally been dismissed as an interlude in Gautier's poetic career, yet in many respects it marks a turning point.[1] *España* in fact describes a progress towards Gautier's relinquishing of the broader romantic forms that is not recorded elsewhere; considered consecutively, a number of its poems articulate the poet's increasing dissatisfaction with the romantic mode.

The mid-nineteenth century in France was an unsettled period for lyric poets in general. The triumph of the romantics encouraged the grandiose and visionary tendencies of the older generation beyond the fifties, but younger poets soon questioned their legacy. Among the more obvious signs of discontent and uncertainty were the reemergence of satire and the appearance of the prose poem.[2] Less obvious indications were increasing doubts about the efficacy of language, these complicated by questions bearing on the subject and subjectivity of the lyric poem. Though some of his poetry might be described as quasi-satirical, Gautier confined himself for the most part to traditional forms of lyric poetry. In the late thirties he experimented with models that reveal him hesitating between two general poetic routes. His efforts tended on the one hand towards the extended meditation, which had appealed to an older generation nurtured on neoclassical diction and noble sentiments. On the other, they tended towards the smaller poem in which the human equation was less apparent and whose audience was as yet uncertain. In *España,* written between 1840 and 1845, the same hesitancy obtains—the poems are generally either discursive or lapidary—but certain of the poems represent a compromise of sorts, and they are more markedly inspired by misgivings that had troubled the poet from the outset.

In *España* these misgivings, complicated by Gautier's longstanding vacillation between despair and euphoria, become focused and intense. In a handful of the poems they are voiced by the silent images of landscape, by mineral visions informing a dialectic that led the poet to question the romantic mode, his own adequacy, and the very possibility of poetry. These poems represent an uneasy union of poetic models peculiar to *España* alone in that they poeticize esthetic debate as well as Gautier's particular unease. They raise issues—in particular the issue of communication—that also preoccupied the Symbolists, whose language would become increasingly indirect and hermetic. As poets moved away from the romantic model, in which description is correlative to argument, they withdrew—or seemed to withdraw—from their poetry. Poetry was increasingly faulted for its impersonality, and Gautier's more than most. However, the case has been made, and will again in these pages be made, for the lyricism of poetry whose complexity of expression gives it the air of an artifact separated from its maker. The poetry of *Emaux et Camées* is in some respects such poetry, exemplifying "the cult of euphony and *le beau vers*...controlled emotion objectified and sustained through the representation of the exterior world" (Houston 18-19). As a result of his experimentation, Gautier's poetry would become increasingly dehumanized according to some, and artificial in the best sense of the word. The same Baudelaire who defended the man of feeling also recognized the poet of "*le non-moi*" (*BOC* 2, 107). The lyricism of Gautier's mature poetry would come to inhere almost exclusively in its form, especially in the effects of "l'épithète musicale," which he had earlier rejected in favor of "l'épithète qui peint."[3]

Chapter I
Gautier *poète*

SINCE THE CRITICAL RESPONSE TO *ESPAÑA* over the years has been largely consistent with reactions to his other efforts, both early and mature, a general review of that response is in order. Most critics have conceded Gautier's lexical knowledge, his visual acuity, and his technical skill, but they are divided in their assessment of him as a lyric poet. Many of his contemporaries complained of a "manque de souffle." Sainte-Beuve, for example, wrote "Ici, chez M. Gautier, l'eau ne court que sous une surface glacée et miroitant au soleil . . . entre vous et le sentiment, au lieu du libre cours s'interpose cette glace d'images ininterrompue et peinte en mille tons" (*RDDM,* September 15, 1838). Yet Baudelaire praised his "immense intelligence innée de la correspondance et du symbolisme universels" (*BOC* 2, 117), and he placed Gautier in the lyric tradition revived by the romantics. Barbey d'Aurevilly was similarly persuaded. In 1862, he wrote of *Emaux et Camées:* "tous ces bijoux . . . ont parfois la vibration fougueuse de disques lancés, et sont teints de sang comme des flèches" (Barbey 1, 237). The controversy surrounding Gautier would continue along these lines. Only recently has closer analysis of the poems tended to support Baudelaire and others of like mind.

During the late nineteenth and early twentieth centuries, Gautier's poetry was praised by those who valued formal rigor. In England Swinburne, who made the major English contribution to the commemorative *Tombeau de Théophile Gautier,* published in 1873, a year after Gautier's death, was perhaps his greatest champion. Gautier's example influenced esthetes such as Pater and Moore, and especially *fin de siècle* decadents such as Symons and Wilde. In the first decades of the twentieth century, Pound and Eliot considered *Emaux et Camées* a corrective to abuses of *le vers libre.* But there were those who deplored in him the absence of a social and historical dimension. Zola complained that Gautier offered "aucune idée nouvelle . . . aucune vérité humaine de quelque profondeur, aucune prescience de l'évolution des siècles" (Tennant 120). Faguet and Lanson followed Sainte-Beuve's example in finding Gautier lacking in sensitivity and "wedded to the object."[1] Such critics subscribed to the romantic notion that the poem should be exemplary, that however idiosyncratic-seeming it might be, its experience should still be of value to all.[2]

Fernand Brunetière was the first of Gautier's compatriots after Baudelaire to offer a more discriminating view of the poet. In his *L'Evolution de la poésie lyrique en France au dix-neuvième siècle* (1894), Brunetière discerns in Gautier a failure to integrate image and idea, and it is this aspect of Gautier's poetry that subsequent detractors have most often fastened upon. He observed, "Il n'y a pas incorporation . . . mais plutôt juxtaposition de l'image et l'idée."[3] A number of critics in fact considered Gautier's preoccupation with surfaces inimical to lyricism; Gide for example unkindly referred to Gautier's "cécité pour tout ce qui n'est pas le monde extérieur" (Gide, *Incidences* 155).[4] The objections here, again, are less to the visual character of Gautier's poetry than to its apparent absence of feeling. Such objections, according to one recent critic, are the result of a "romantisme foncier dont la mentalité moderne, malgré tout, ne s'est pas vraiment détachéé" (Tortonese 80). The notion of mood as externalized, as divorced from *le moi* and generated by objects alone, was slow to impose itself.

Henri van der Tuin (*L'Evolution psychologique, esthétique et littéraire de Théophile Gautier*), writing in the early thirties, was the first to propose a theory of the man behind the "unlyrical" poems. For him, Gautier's psychology explains the problematic subjectivity of his poetry as well as the poetics of *Emaux et Camées,* of which he writes: "Dans le développement de cette dernière forme de métrique chez Gautier, nous voyons surtout une influence de la vie intérieure" (Van der Tuin 266). Van der Tuin discerns in Gautier a "pauvreté d'invention," which he attributes to passivity and lack of vitality (46). These he believes to be in the main responsible for the "weaknesses"—particularly in Gautier's early poetry—described by Brunetière and Gabriel Brunet.[5] Van der Tuin, then, reveals a man of feeling, applauding the "unlyrical" Gautier for whom form would have been a defense against sentiment rather than evidence of it, as Baudelaire had maintained ("Ce que vous appelez indifférence n'est que la résignation du désespoir" [*BOC* 2, 128]). Whichever the case, both observers concede the influence of "feeling," and it would not much matter whether the octosyllabic line were therapy or symptom.

The 1960s, during which Gautier attracted the attention of a number of modern readers, few of them sympathetic,[6] added little to earlier criticism of Gautier's poetry. In 1963 Raymond Giraud commented, "Théophile Gautier's stock has fallen off considerably in the last half-century and it is unlikely that any efforts to rehabilitate him will be wholly successful" (Giraud, "Dehumanization" 3-4). He conceded the influence of Gautier's conception of poetry on the artistic consciousness of the twentieth century, yet considered his descriptive technique "dehumanizing," agreeing with Prévost that the artisan in Gautier left the poet in the shadow. Here again, the notion of lyricism as centered in *le moi* continued to foster a narrow view of lyric poetry. Georges Poulet (1966) and Michel Crouzet (1972) reiterate earlier critical positions in their analysis of Gautier's "art de surface."[7] Poulet describes the process by which Gautier is led to the surface of things,[8] while Crouzet criticizes Gautier's overreliance on formal models.[9] Neither Poulet nor Crouzet see beyond Gautier's fixation on appearances and surfaces, and both attribute his "superficiality" to the poet's painterly instincts, as Brunet had done almost a century earlier.[10] Finally, Léon Cellier predicted of Gautier that "ce n'est pas le poète qui a des chances de survivre" (Cellier, "Présentation" 580).

In his *Théophile Gautier* (1975), a slim but comprehensive and thoroughly documented study, P. E. Tennant reviews earlier opinions with a view to setting Gautier's *œuvre* in proper perspective. His analyses of Gautier's poetry, particularly his demonstrations of Gautier's technical skill, provide an unprecedented synthesis of the poet's accomplishments. Tennant examines the whole range of Gautier's poetry in a social and ideological context. He attributes the poet's final preference for the octosyllabic verse form to the critical position he had always espoused: his belief in the autonomy of art, his rejection of utility and his tendency to regard art as artifact. He also, like van der Tuin, regards Gautier's eventual *esthétique* as a response to "the immediate external context on the one hand and to temperamental and psychological factors on the other" (Tennant 100), and his poetry the poetry of one isolated and alienated from his society. He is perhaps the first to discuss at any length the implications of Gautier's sense of inadequacy for his poetics, maintaining that it was generalized, influenced both by aesthetic theory and contemporary social and political circumstances (100-101).[11]

Tennant contends that Gautier's own response was extreme, and that his art became a desperate therapy, a deliberately irresponsible and subversive art "crystallising around certain interrelated attitudes: . . . a tendency to introspection leading to narcissism, dandyism and dilettantism on the one hand, the urge to depersonalise and materialise responses in the cult of the artificial on the other" (101-2). He quotes Gautier himself on the subject: "Faced with his ideal, the artist experiences 'le sentiment de l'impuissance relative à son art,' causing 'l'incurable mélancolie et l'inquiétude sans trêve des grands hommes.' "[12] These words describe a situation daunting to all artists, but they also reveal a condition peculiar to himself, a sense of inadequacy born of a fear of the amorphous totality of life, the consequence of which was his abandoning the effort to communicate with the broader public. Tennant concludes that Gautier's poetry is "turned not outwards, to 'connect,' but inwards, to share with a coterie of connaisseurs an essentially contemplative act involving a wide-ranging divertissement" (99). Tennant was one of the first observers to demonstrate Gautier's affinities with the Symbolist poets, especially the musical element of his romances and his imagery of arrested movement, evoking life mysteriously poised between the animate and inanimate (111-13).

Other critics have also addressed the issue of Gautier's "art de surface." Harry Cockerham, editor of the 1973 edition of Gautier's *Poésies,* was one of the first to recognize Gautier's tendency to externalize and objectify emotion. He notes, "It is rarely in fact quite so easy to separate description from lyricism in Gautier's poetry" (Cockerham 28). Commenting on Gautier's early poems, Cockerham submits that "Description itself has become confession, and is imbued with the poet's own attitudes. . . . The description does not try to be complete or exhaustive: it is on the contrary selective and condensed to the point where it acquires a symbolic value" (29). Serge Fauchereau points to the musician and Symbolist in Gautier in his *Théophile Gautier* (Fauchereau 67-69),[13] and in his penetrating analysis of *Emaux et Camées,* Clive Scott has made a similar case for Gautier's poetry. He contends that since the octosyllable is devoid of segmentational imperatives, it permits a double rhythmic perspective that in turn gives it "a fluid, mobile, undefined surface which plants it squarely in the flux of relativity and change." For this reason, he adds, "it is impossible to agree with those who find in Gautier's octosyllables the deft, crisp outlines of the plastic model" (Scott 34).[14] Scott also quarrels with those who regard Gautier's descriptive art as limiting: "The reader is invited into the poem, to see not so much what the poet sees as what the poet's description allows him to see or encourages him to see; the bareness or laconicness of the observations are precisely what creates around all objects an envelope of interpretive freedom and allows the infiltration of personal association" (42).[15] E. G. Lien, like Cockerham, also appreciates the subjectivity of much of Gautier's poetry. Of the poems inspired by travel he wrote in 1991 that the poetic voyage "upon which we embark is at once a geographical displacement and an itinerant exploration of the poet's psyche. . . . The poet's imagination . . . transforms his description of the voyage in such a way that the presented exterior world materializes his various states of mind" (Lien 51). Gautier himself had said "le paysage est dans moi-même" (Spoelberch de Lovenjoul xvii).

Constance Gosselin-Schick's *Seductive Resistance: The Poetry of Théophile Gautier* offers a modern analysis of Gautier *poète*. Gosselin-Schick posits a readership that has found Gautier's poetry wanting over the years because it escapes classification. She maintains that the poems have been misunderstood because they have been judged largely on the basis of their referentiality and dismissed for their want of sincerity and profundity. She proposes a reading "which accepts the disguise of Gautier's writing, its displacement and its artifice, in short its textuality. . . . What needs to be done for Gautier is to acknowledge this artifice and/or artificiality not as something negative, something that goes against or prevents 'good,' 'authentic' poetry, but as an essential constituent of poeticity" (Gosselin-Schick 4-5). Defining beauty as "the triumph of the nothingness of appearance over the nothingness of the real," she contends that Gautier's nonessential and gratuitous surfaces are intended to demonstrate the failure of poetry: "His poetry is a chiseled, polished surface which reveals its hollowness and inadequacy" (6).

These large claims are brought to bear on the whole corpus of Gautier's poetry. Gosselin-Schick represents many of Gautier's poems as negations of themselves that point to other poems rather than as poems in their own right. She makes an excellent case for the poem as illusion, particularly when, like *Albertus,* it is playful, parodic, and tongue-in-cheek. It is other than what it is: " 'Thébaïde' constructs itself by evoking or simulating what it would not be and makes this otherness significant of what it would be" (67). And it is true that Gautier's obsessive nihilism occasionally led him to indulge in paradox, to write poetry of the sort that appears to negate itself. But such a view, which often disregards the effects of diction, image, and rhythm, is unprofitably reductive. Furthermore, it tends to deny rather than affirm, and it is doubtful that the artisan in Gautier would never have conceded presence to an art that meant more to him than any other.

There are as we have seen a growing number of readers of Gautier's poetry whose major efforts, in fact, have been to define the quality of that presence, particularly in his later work, but none to date has considered the role of *España* in this regard. With the exception of Jasinski's *'L'España' de Théophile Gautier,* which is primarily concerned with the accuracy of Gautier's representations, the poetry of his middle years has not inspired a book-length study. At first reading the collection appears to offer nothing markedly different from his earlier efforts; its interest is superficially thematic: the journey through Spain from the dark north to the sunny south paralleled by the progressive relinquishing of romantic poetic models. Yet this small volume, written between 1840 and 1845, was inspired by Gautier's effort to confirm a definitive poetics, an effort that was both difficult and protracted, and it documents the evolution of Gautier's art during its most critical stages. The poems of *España* are evidence of his having abandoned an expansive lyric model for one whose lyricism was tempered by formal constraints. What is less obvious are the doubts that determined the progress of this transition, doubts that had troubled the writer from the beginning of his poetic career. A review of Gautier's early poetry is therefore in order.

Gautier in the 1830s

The year 1830, which confirmed the triumph of the romantics—in which the pink-vested Gautier as a defender of Hugo's revolutionary drama *Hernani* played a celebrated part—also witnessed the demise of romanticism in its purest form. Two tendencies or "schools," had emerged: "l'école intime," whose principles were exemplified in Lamartine's *Méditations* (1820), Hugo's *Odes* (1822-26) and especially in Sainte-Beuve's *Joseph Delorme* (1829), and "l'école pittoresque," for which Hugo's *Les Orientales* (1829) provided the cornerstone. The poets of "l'école intime," inspired in part by the contemporaneity and popular appeal of George Sand's novels, advocated the expression of commonplace feelings rather than exalted emotions, whereas "l'école pittoresque" sought more exotic subjects in its new emphasis upon the visual and concrete. This *matérialisme* impressed the critical establishment as a radical departure from traditional poetics, though the *tendance pittoresque* had been latent in French lyric poetry since the Renaissance. Sainte-Beuve was in fact the first to determine its origins in the tenets of the Pléiade.[16]

The principles of "l'école pittoresque" were dramatically manifest in Hugo's *Les Orientales,* though Hugo would soon embark upon a more ambitious poetics. Colors, sonorities, and rhythms combined to produce a variety of sensations long absent from French lyric poetry. The conservative critics of "la vieille école" joined with the older romantics in their denunciation of a violence and sensuality they perceived as debased. It was *Les Orientales* and specifically its "Préface," that became the bible for the Petit Cénacle, the younger generation of French poets. This confraternity of Hugo's disciples, which included among their number Nerval and Gautier, lived their new credo together flamboyantly, no doubt partly in opposition to the pious missionary spirit of "l'école intime."[17]

What is curious is that the new credo inspired relatively little poetry in the twenty years that followed. The older romantic poets continued to write sporadically, but their poetry tended to be visionary and didactic. Lamartine, who served as Député from 1833 to 1851, would write poetry inspired by social and patriotic ideals during those years. The later poetry of Vigny and Hugo, equally optimistic, would also celebrate social reform and progress. Hugo wrote no poetry at all in the years between *Les Rayons et les Ombres* (1840) and *Les Contemplations* (1856). The literary climate in the 1830s, which saw the appearance of the great novels of Stendhal (*Le Rouge et le noir* [1831], *La Chartreuse de Parme* [1839]) and Balzac (*Le Père Goriot* [1835], *Eugénie Grandet* [1833]), seemed more favorable to prose. Leconte de Lisle, Nerval, and Baudelaire would not produce their major efforts until after 1852, the year that Gautier's *Emaux et Camées* was published. Gautier and Théodore de Banville, also a precursor of the Parnassians, were the only major poets to publish collections of poems during the 1840s. Gautier, then, wrote his volume of Spanish poems during a kind of poetic drought. He had only his earlier mentors and himself to look to.

Gautier's Early Poems

The appearance in 1830 of Gautier's first volume of poems, *Poésies*, was, as he himself observed, ill-timed. The poet who was trying his wings had to contend not only with the events of 1830—with the *bouleversement* of the July Monarchy—but also with the conservative critical establishment whose attention was drawn more to Hugo and other poets than to the relatively unknown Gautier. The volume published in 1830 was consequently withdrawn. It was republished in 1832 along with "Préface," twenty new poems, "Poésies diverses," and *Albertus*, the title poem. *La Comédie de la mort* was published in 1838, along with a number of shorter poems from "*Poésies diverses*." Gautier's *Poésies complètes,* published in 1845, is composed of the preceding poems and *Poésies nouvelles*, which includes *España* and *Pièces diverses*.[18]

The response to Gautier's early poems, which exemplify tendencies of both the "école intime" and the "école pittoresque," was generally dismissive. Critics fastened almost exclusively upon their derivative nature, upon Gautier's borrowings from older French, German, and English poets, and René Jasinski points to numerous echoes of Lamartine, Hugo, Sainte-Beuve, Musset, Byron, and Heine.[19] Gautier, of course, made no secret of his borrowings, considering them a kind of homage paid to those he regarded as his mentors. In fact, he was usually given to naming his sources, even in the poems themselves.[20] In his earliest poems are also to be found a number of innovations encouraged by the early romantics: rich rhyme, the *vers cassé,* enjambement, and diversity of color, to name but a few. What would set Gautier apart from his contemporaries in his early efforts was the art of his *microcosmes,* a genre, or better notion, borrowed from Goethe.[21] These are serene visions that transform the natural world into theater, exploiting a complex of techniques through which experience is materialized and miniaturized. In these *microcosmes* the lyricism that would characterize Gautier's mature poetry—albeit in a more refined form—is already apparent, for example in "Lamento," and "Chant du Grillon," not to mention the poems set to music by Berlioz. Though he experimented with a variety of poetic models, Gautier's early poetry is generally celebrative or pessimistic. His darker poems, though imitative of romantic models, are inspired largely by a nihilism peculiar to Gautier alone,[22] which was ignored by critics who denounced the derivative—and especially the gothic—element in *Poésies.*[23]

Poésies

Gautier's "Préface" to the 1832 edition of *Poésies* helps to clarify his earliest ambitions. It suggests that his first efforts would be discreet rather than sensational or grandiose:

> Ce sont d'abord de petits intérieurs d'un effet doux et calme, de petits paysages à la manière des Flamands, d'une touche tranquille, d'une couleur un peu étouffée, ni grandes montagnes, ni perspectives à perte de vue, ni torrents, ni cataractes. (*PC* 1, 83-84)

This first section of the "Préface" alerts the reader to the modest rural character of the poems and to the importance of *"le monde extérieur."* These small poems are characterized by a concentration upon small things and by a *précieux* naiveté that would recur in his later poems. The "Préface" to the 1832 edition of his first efforts reveals, however, that Gautier was not yet wholly determined on the path that would lead to *Emaux et Camées*. Though he preferred shorter verse forms, there were times when he would adopt the grand manner and venture into legend and myth, describing broader panoramas. These poems reveal preoccupations uncongenial to his tiny Edens, and they suggest that for Gautier mood determined form. Whereas the *microcosmes* are luminous, his longer narrative poems—often one extended stanza composed of alexandrines—tend to be dark. Their sentiments are commonplace and typical of the older generation of romantics. With the exception of *Albertus,* this is the poetry of romantic posturing, of autumn landscapes, and gothic horrors.

There are a few poems in this collection, however, that are less easily classified. These reveal Gautier's interest in experimenting with a variety of formal models, and they raise questions, inspired by Gautier's recurrent pessimism and by uncertainties about himself. Their context tends accordingly to be gothic and they are often articulated in mineral images—tombs, churches, and the like. In this respect they adumbrate the poetry of *España,* in which such misgivings would become more focused. "Ballade" (*PC* 1, 55), for example, joins the *matière* of the *microcosme* to a daydream disturbed by the appearance of death in the form of a romantic cliché, the merciless hunter. This quasi-idyllic poem looks forward to others in which Gautier proposes the unwritten poem as the ideal poem, the fruit of contemplation, that is to say, of inaction. "Sonnet III," also a meditation on death, proposes an image that will recur in the poems of 1838 and in *España:* the mineral structure that simultaneously encloses, protects, embraces, and crushes. Here the lush music of the initial illusion persists in the tercets that dispel it as the amorous "*regard enchanteur*" is sustained in the "lierre qui . . . embrasse" (*PC* 1, 63). The mineral image will become equivocal, even polyvalent, as in "Un Vers de Wordsworth," where the church spire ("—Clochers silencieux montrant du doigt le ciel" [*PC* 1, 118]) has a number of connotations, among them the safeguarding of an ideal and hollowness, as well as hallowedness. In these early poems Gautier sports with death, gives it life, and immortalizes it in its most imperishable symbol, in the sacred stone of church and tomb, and in the poem itself. In later poems he would continue to play with these notions, but the mineral figure would evolve to accommodate the expression of something more personal in *España*.

The Ironic Gautier: *Albertus*

According to the "Préface" to Gautier's 1832 edition of the *Poésies, Albertus* was to represent the final stage of an evolution. His analogy, borrowed from the drawing studio, is playful:

> A mesure que l'on avance, le dessin devient plus ferme, les méplats se font sentir, les os prennent de la saillie, et l'on aboutit à la légende semi-diabolique, semi-fashionable, qui a nom *Albertus,* et qui donne le titre au volume, comme la pièce la plus importante et la plus actuelle du recueil. (*PC* 1, 83-84)

Gautier's gothic poem, like his introduction to it, is very much tongue-in-cheek. It is Gautier's satire of *le bas romantisme,* in which his coarser instincts are given full rein. A long poem consisting of 122 twelve-line stanzas, *Albertus* is more ambitious than any of the earlier poems, if only by virtue of its theme—the idealist destroyed by his pursuit of the absolute—and of the broad range of romantic conventions that it simultaneously indulges and parodies. What is of interest in *Albertus* for an understanding of *España* is not only the broader argument of the piece, that is, the quest for the absolute, but also the poem's teasing and irreverence. Gautier rejected *le rire* in poetry, but he did not reject play.[24] *Albertus* is also stylistically more daring; it stands with *Les Orientales* as a corrective both to romantic excess and to neoclassical stodginess.[25] In this respect it is an early example of Gautier's anti-romantic tendency and of his experimentation with new modes. After 1842, the year in which Gautier definitively abandoned the expanded romantic model, playfulness, albeit a far more discreet playfulness, would become an integral part of his poetics.

Poésies diverses: *La Comédie de la mort*

Gautier's nihilism continued to dominate his poetry in the late thirties, but it was complicated by fear of personal failure. In his preface to *Albertus*, he had described himself as one of many unfortunates: "Cependant, si éloigné qu'il soit des choses de la vie, il sait que le vent ne souffle pas à la poésie; il sent parfaitement toute l'inopportunité d'une pareille publication; pourtant, il ne craint pas de jeter entre deux émeutes, peut-être entre deux pestes, un volume purement littéraire" (*PC* 1, 81-82). The likelihood that the relative obscurity he continued to experience was circumstantial did not much comfort him, and the poet of the late thirties nourished misgivings that would preoccupy him for some time to come. *La Comédie de la mort*, published along with *Poésies diverses* in 1838, is the last major poem Gautier wrote before he left for Spain in the summer of 1840. It is a philosophical and poetic excursion reminiscent of the romantic *épopée* and of Dante's *Inferno*. Jasinski writes of the poem:

> Aussi marque-t-il une étape importante. Il reflète la crise intérieure que traverse alors Gautier, et dont *Mademoiselle de Maupin* fixe les paroxysmes les plus violents: élans déçus, reploiements douloureux, funèbres hantises, nihilisme enfin, alternent

ici avec les poussées d'une vitalité puissante jusqu'à l'affermissement sur un fond pessimiste d'une véritable sensualisme esthétique, altéré de lumière et révolté contre la mort. (*PC* 1, xxxvii)

The poem, inspired by what the poet referred to as a juvenile *maladie gothique* (Bergerat 13), relies heavily upon mineral impedimenta, and it is unusually intense. Its prologue, "Portail," is composed in terza rima, which propels the nascent poem—this a conglomeration of floating coffins, ships, and cathedrals—towards two exploratory sections: "La Vie dans la mort" and "La Mort dans la vie," each composed of six-line stanzas. In "Portail" the poet is a gambler of sorts who throws his ships (his poems) onto the seas like dice onto the gaming table; the ocean will swallow them but they will rise "hardiment comme des cathédrales," if *Dieu* will visit them. In "La Vie dans la mort" the poem relates a dialogue between "la Trépassée" and "le ver," concluding with the grim comfort of "Console-toi,—La mort donne la vie" (*PC* 2,17) and a vision of Raphael fulminating against the effects of scientific progress upon art. "La Mort dans la vie" reviews the dramas of Faust and don Juan in the form of a dialectic voiced by these two figures and completed by Napoleon. All three affirm the futility of their separate quests and testify to the vanity of all human endeavor.

Its nihilistic message notwithstanding, *La Comédie de la mort* parades a dense and sumptuous plasticity before the reader's eyes. As he does in *Albertus,* Gautier exploits the theatricality of an abundance of gothic necrophilia, and there is a pervasive irony in at least some of its episodes. Its premises are commonplace, and the melodramatic context of Napoleon's unlikely remorse (the use of "LUI" and "L'HOMME," for example) suggests that the poet's tongue may have been in his cheek as it was in *Albertus,* and there is even at times a bit of frank humor ("Les squelettes tâchaient de rajuster leurs têtes" [*PC* 2, 42]). The poem is a grandiose variation on the theme of earlier poems that propose the poem as the immortal form of the perishable, for example, of "l'anémone frêle" as well as of "le cypress" (*PC* 1, 3), and the game-playing persists until the end, often as double-talk:

> Je ne suis plus, hélas! que l'ombre de moi-même,
> Que la tombe vivante où gît tout ce que j'aime,
>   Et je me survis seul;
> Je promène avec moi les dépouilles glacées
> De mes illusions, charmantes trépassées
>   Dont je suis le linceul. (*PC* 2, 46)

The closing section, in which even his muse fails him, is a last appeal that is simultaneously moving and ironic.[26]

However qualified, the nihilism of *La Comédie de la mort* points, as Jasinski suggests, to a state of unease if not to an impending crisis: the poet's bitter and often violent pronouncements are hardly the product of philosophical detachment. Here mineral structures—tombs and the like—figure as problematic antidotes to universal death and decay. The poet perceives of his poems, for example, as floating vaults, preserving paradoxically what no longer exists: "Mes vers sont les tombeaux tout brodés de sculptures / . . . / Chacun est le cercueil d'une illusion morte" (*PC* 2, 6).[27] These equations would come to play a more complex role, notably in the poetry of *España*. Mineral substances—the lapidary model, the poem as prism—had figured in Gautier's early poetry but not in support of extended debate. The larger structures of *La Comédie de la mort* are the prototype of monoliths that would increasingly inform the arguments of Gautier's prose and his poetry as equivocal analogues of achievement and immortality.

Poésies diverses: "Ténèbres" and "La Thébaïde"

Many of the figures in *La Comédie de la mort* are present in *Poésies diverses*. A number of these poems are celebrative, especially those that experiment with more complex forms. But the subject of frustrated ambition (*la gloire*) recurs in many of the poems or in sections of poems, and mineral imagery, in particular the mineral structure as it is related to the poetic enterprise, figures increasingly in the texts and subtexts of others. "Le Triomphe de Pétrarque" (1836) names the Italian poet the most enviable success. In "Dédain" the poet concedes the power of ambition, whereas in "Elégie" he concludes that "toute ambition meurt aux bras d'une femme" (*PC* 2, 205). Mineral imagery has now become pervasive: one can cite the armature of "L'Hippopotame," the marble of "Niobe," of "Cariatides," and of "Le Sphinx." Two poems are devoted to the cathedral: "Notre Dame" and "Le Sommet de la tour." In the first the edifice is the analogue of the poem ("Et le Seigneur habite en toi. / Monde de poésie" [*PC* 1, 52]). In the second it has become a metaphor for the stages of the poet's career, but he is no longer confident: "Du haut de cette tour à grand'peine achevée, / Pourrai-je t'entrevoir, perspective rêvée, / Terre de Chanaan où tendait mon effort?" (*PC* 1, 215).[28] "Ténèbres" and "La Thébaïde" point to the seven years of silence that would elapse between Gautier's writing of *España* and *Emaux et Camées*.

In "Ténèbres," a bleak poem also composed in terza rima, Gautier's preoccupation with *la gloire* persists: "Il faut un grand génie avec un bonheur rare / Pour faire jusqu'au ciel monter son monument, / Et de ce double don le destin est avare" (*PC* 2, 60), adding at the end of the poem, in response perhaps to the question posed at the end of "Portail": "Le Dieu ne viendra pas. L'Eglise est renversée" (*PC* 2, 64). "Thébaïde" (1837) anticipates both the literal desert Gautier would cross in 1840 and the symbolic wasteland of 1842. In this poem of death and dessication, the poet's emotions are uncharacteristically intense: "Du temple de mon âme, il ne reste debout / Que deux piliers d'airain, la haine et le dégoút" (71). "Thébaïde," however, anticipates exile and renewal:

Mon rêve le plus cher et le plus caressé,
. . . .
C'est de m'ensevelir au fond d'une chartreuse,
Dans une solitude inabordable, affreuse;
. . . . Dans quelque Sierra
. . . .
Dans l'immobilité savourer lentement,
Comme un philtre endormeur, l'anéantissement:
. . . .
Je veux dans le néant renouveler mon être,
M'isoler de moi-même et ne plus me connaître. (*PC* 2, 65-67)[29]

Gautier's early poetry, then, prepares us to some extent for *España*. A number of tendencies apparent in the poems of the thirties would help determine the direction Gautier's poetics would take: his recurrent nihilism and the polarization of mood it engendered, his painterly orientation—especially his fixation upon minerals—and a related interest in experimenting with shorter and more complex poetic forms, and finally, the need for recognition. During the mid to late thirties, when his life was at its most unsettled and before he set out for Spain, Gautier had yet to make his way. Many of his early poems are those of an innovator, to be sure, but there are many that demonstrate his reluctance to abandon the romantic model, doubtless because it still found favor with a broad reading public. Readers had applauded his critical aphorisms rather than his poems, but Gautier's most cherished wish was to succeed as a poet. Jasinski observes: "Critique, on le craignait. Poète, on le contestait toujours, et la déception était pour lui cruelle" (Jasinski, *L'España* 271). It was in part his perceived failure to sustain a lofty theme[30] and to reach a broader public that led him to revise his poetics, and the months in Spain would prove crucial to that process.

Chapter II

The Journey to Spain

The Appeal of Spain in the early 1800s; the precursors of Gautier's *Voyage en Espagne*

THE FRENCH WERE NOT MUCH INCLINED to visit Spain until the nineteenth century. Until well into the eighteenth century, travel to Spain had been sporadic and infrequent, undertaken by those assigned with specific ecclesiastical, commercial, military, or diplomatic missions. Spain's rise to power in the sixteenth century stimulated the admiration and curiosity of the French, but its decline in the seventeenth had the opposite effect.[1] The general impetus to travel sparked by the "querelle des anciens et des modernes" and fueled by Enlightenment cosmopolitanism did not encourage the French—perhaps even more reluctant because of Voltaire's and Montesquieu's contempt for "the barbarous country"—to venture beyond the Pyrénées. French tourists in fact did not appear in Spain much before 1820. A number of factors contributed to encourage French tourism around that time: the political rapprochement of France and Spain after the expedition of the Duc d'Angoulême in 1823, the increased awareness in France of Spanish culture resulting from the presence of Spanish *émigrés* and from the importation of Spanish art, and the emergence of a class of people who could afford to travel for pleasure.[2] By the 1820s "le génie espagnol" had firmly impressed itself upon the French. They were now more inclined to risk the dangers and discomforts of Spanish highways and to dismiss the charge of barbarity leveled at Spain by the Enlightenment, a charge reinforced by exaggerated reports of brutality from survivors of the Napoleonic campaigns. Moreover, Italy, Germany and England had ceased to be strange; they were well traveled and no longer attracted the adventurous.

The Appeal of Spain to Gautier

In May of 1840, Gautier was approaching his thirties. The literary climate a decade after Louis-Philippe's accession to the throne was far from the exhilarating one it had been in 1830. The jubilation of *Hernani* had long since subsided and the *Petit Cénacle* had been dispersed for some years. Gautier had published a variety of literary efforts: his first *Poésies, Albertus, Les Jeunes-France, Les Grotesques, Mademoiselle de Maupin, La Comédie de la mort,* several short stories, and reviews of literature, art, and the performing arts. He had for some years been employed as a dramatic critic for the *Chronique de Paris,* a position he had obtained with Balzac's help. When his friend Eugène Piot proposed a trip to Spain in search of art treasures made available through the dissolution and despoiling of monasteries during the civil war, Gautier accepted with enthusiasm. It is no secret that in setting out to Spain in 1840 with Piot, Gautier sought to escape from Paris, from the tedium of his journalistic assignments, and from his domestic responsibilities.

But there were other reasons. He now had the opportunity to see firsthand the country that had so fascinated the *Jeunes-France.* They envisioned Spain as a land of extreme contrasts, moral and material. It was a land where barbarity coexisted with sophistication, austerity with luxury, a land that had produced the Inquisition as well as the Andalusian serenade. *Le Petit Cénacle* was consequently drawn to Spanish painting—examples of which Gautier would have seen in Louis-Philippe's Musée Espagnol—because it expressed these contrasts visually in intense and vibrant color. Moreover, it epitomized the newly formulated romantic principle of the *mélange des contraires,* that is, the mingling of the sublime and the grotesque.[3] It is understandable, given Gautier's painterly orientation, and especially his enthusiastic responses to the Musée Espagnol, that he should want to see Spain for himself. The trip lasted five months and took the two men by various horse- and mule-drawn conveyances from Irun through Burgos to Madrid, then south to Andalusia and the cities of Grenada, Málaga, Córdoba, and Seville, and then northward by boat from Cádiz to Barcelona with brief visits to cities on the coast. Unfortunately, the expedition was financially ruinous to Gautier.

French Accounts of Travel to Spain; Gautier's *Voyage en Espagne*

There was a proliferation of literary works inspired by travel to Spain during the early part of the century. The travel accounts were generally undistinguished and limited in scope, confined to descriptions of one city or region. Most of them were memoirs penned by survivors of the Napoleonic campaigns or by French physicians who had come to Barcelona in 1820 to offer their assistance to victims of the plague of that year. Still others had been inspired by the expedition of the Duc d'Angoulême in 1823 to help reestablish the monarchy of Ferdinand VII. The more extensive *récits de voyage* tended to follow one of two established traditions, the one scholarly, the other imaginative. The former would include Louis Viardot's *Etudes sur l'histoire des institutions, de la littérature, du théâtre et des beaux-arts* (1835), which corrected many erroneous and long-held views of Spain. An example of the latter are the memoirs of Antoine Fontaney ("Lord John Feeling"), *Scènes de la vie castillane et andalouse* (1835), which are so exaggeratedly romantic as to suggest parody. They are fictions that perpetuate the myths of Spanish arrogance, cruelty and vengefulness. In the 1820s and 1830s travel writers appeared to be divided into two camps: those bent on destroying the Spain of legend and those determined to preserve it.

Towards the middle of the century, travel writers had to some extent reconciled the two approaches in their emphasis upon the purely visual aspect of the journey, which was in keeping with the literary trend towards the *pittoresque*. The romantics' efforts to broaden and diversify the subjects of their novels and poetry had resulted in a lexical expansion of the language, and writers now disposed of a richer vocabulary to describe the physical world. The new emphasis was also in part a reaction against the more sentimental memoirists' failure to see and their scholarly counterparts' failure to enjoy. The former had appealed too much to the imagination, the latter too little. Unlike Dumas, who often forces Spain to conform to his own romantic notions, Gautier and Mérimée would focus upon "ces mille petits détails que les voyageurs négligent pour de grandes considérations poétiques que l'on peut très-bien écrire sans aller dans le pays" (*VE* 23). They would combine accuracy with visual stimulation. Margaret Williams observes: "The increasing tendency to regard Spain . . . as a vast painting unrolled before the artist makes itself seen not only in the text of travel books, but also in the prolific illustrations found in most books towards the end of the century. The corresponding change in verbal descriptions stresses the dictates of fashion that the writer should adopt more and more the attitudes of an artist who stands aloof from his creation, so that not even his shadow comes between the work and its public" (Williams 151).

The difficulty in formulating a theory of the romantic *récit de voyage* in the early to mid-nineteenth century lies in separating it both from accounts that tend towards the guide or study and from those that tend towards romantic fictions. There is often a good deal of subjectivity in the first category and a considerable amount of factual documentation in the second. What sets the romantic *récit de voyage* apart from both, as exemplified in the travel narratives of Chateaubriand, is its chronicling not of one, but of two journeys, the one literal, the other figurative. The genre is both factual and, and as Michel Butor has put it, "*livresque*"[4]—bookish or literary. It is factual in its reportage of events and physical details. It is literary in its affinity to epic and romance, and in the complex devices that bind the literal journey to the spiritual adventure.[5] The absence of a sustained symbolic journey in the narratives of Viardot and Fontaney eliminates them as simultaneously real and imaginative. With travel books such as Gautier's *Voyage en Espagne* and, for example, Nerval's *Voyage en Orient*,[6] the genre begins to combine the guide with the "voyage sentimental," avoiding the pedantry of the one and the emotional self-indulgence of the other. Gautier was neither a "voyageur géomètre" nor a "Childe Harold," but something in between. He saw Spain through the eyes of a painter, as Williams has observed, but his recordings are not clinically impartial and objective (Williams 360). The shadows cast in *Voyage en Espagne* are what qualify it as a romantic *récit de voyage*.

Voyage en Espagne and *España*

While in Spain, Gautier was to send running commentaries (*feuilletons*) of his travels back to *La Presse, La Revue de Paris,* and *La Revue des Deux Mondes,* whose readership would welcome news of a country still largely unknown to them. These would eventually be assembled first under the title of *Tra-los-Montes* in 1843, and finally as *Voyage en Espagne.* In the spring of 1840, however, Gautier was preoccupied with concerns other than simple curiosity and the desire for change, and his *récit de voyage* would prove to be far more than a readable and informative record of his travels. As we have seen, his spirits had been dampened by the negative critical response to his first volumes of poetry.[7] Moreover, as has also been noted, his disposition had long been complicated by a gloom that was both temperamental and metaphysical. There were in effect two Gautiers. The first was "le bon Théo," the champion of the romantic revolution and Hugo's "plus fanatique séide," the believer in a poetic "microcosm," the genial parodist of "Albertus," and the outspoken apologist for art in *Mademoiselle de Maupin*. This was the exuberant wit, the poet of affirmation. But there was also the man afflicted by a morbid sensibility—a "hantise du néant."[8] Gautier had reached a point in his career where his immediate situation and his longstanding pessimism had joined forces with a growing sense of creative inadequacy. Together they would provoke the crisis that is central to both *Voyage en Espagne* and *España*.[9]

That crisis is veiled in the travel narrative as it is in the poetry. The narrator of *Voyage en Espagne* generally assumes the roles of reporter, guide, critic, and satirist. In most of these he appears detached, venturing his opinion briefly and succinctly and often affecting a genial and witty persona—that of "le bon Théo." The subterranean narrator takes refuge in objectivity and is more elusive ("Je me suis refugié dans le descriptif, certain de ne choquer personne" [*Quand on Voyage,* 139]). As in *España*, there are two dialogues: the first a spirited conversation that the narrator-guide carries on with the reader, the second an argument that the poet sustains with himself and that is articulated in his descriptions. The symbolic journey of *Voyage en Espagne,* then, is the story of a crisis resolved by the narrator's changing vision of his art.

The narrator-guide honors both the Spain of legend and the Spain of 1840. The poet reconciles Spanish art, epitomized for him in the sculpture and architecture of the Spain of the past, to the dynamism of living Spain. In the process he liberates himself from the tyranny of earlier models and from his self-imposed esthetic, constructing his own edifices from the raw materials of the journey. The question "Qu'est-ce qu'une mince feuille de papier à côté d'une montagne de granit?" (*VE* 39) is one of several the narrator will put to himself in the course of his travels that raise the question of his own power to produce a work as enduring as the monuments he beholds. The artist's difficulty is reflected in the disjunction of modes—of the reverential and the comic—that occur in the early pages of the récit. His evocations tend to be of two kinds: they describe either religious art and architecture or his experiences on the road. Gautier regarded these subjects at first as antithetical: the cathedrals were immobile and sublime, the society of the Spanish wayside inn—*la venta*—animated and comic. In the early stages of his journey finished artifacts appear to the narrator as perfect but inhibiting. Though eulogistic, Gautier's early descriptions of Spanish Gothic tend accordingly to express the inert rather than the lively. They are less inventive than the accounts of his adventures on the road, in which he exploits the many resources of his comic genius. His accounts of his experiences—with people, meals, accommodations, transportation, and the weather—raise the ordinary misadventures of the traveler to the level of high comedy; they are dynamic, inventive, often hyperbolic. As the party progresses south, these modes are gradually integrated to one another, the exuberance of the traveler prevailing over the inhibitions of the artist. His evocations of Spanish art become more animated and playful, whereas those of living Spain are increasingly complex, their comedy more refined.

The *récit de voyage* helps to illuminate the poetry. Though as genres *España* and *Voyage en Espagne* are not closely related; both were written during a difficult time in Gautier's life, and one can compare them broadly as responses to a crisis. The traveler's vacillations between depression and elation described in the *feuilletons* written before 1842 roughly parallel those reflected in the poems of *España* composed before that year.[10] The preoccupations of the narrator of *Voyage en Espagne* are similar to those of the poet. There is the same general opposition between the enduring and the ephemeral. Stone—here architecture—as a metaphor for verbal art had the same implications for the *feuilletoniste* as for the poet. The prose writer was awestruck by the Spanish cathedral, but he found its grandeur difficult to transpose; like the poet, he exalted the properties of sculpture but was at the same time inhibited by the finished artifact and the specter of the uncut mineral block. There is also in both works an inclination to experiment, to mingle genres, and with that an increasing playfulness. Gautier's later evocations in *Voyage en Espagne* and in *España* rely less upon the plastic qualities of his subjects and more upon his sense of their dynamic, or better, their theatrical potential. An examination of those sections in *Voyage en Espagne* composed about the same time as the poems will accordingly precede the discussion of the poems themselves.

Chapter III
España

ESPAÑA IN ITS PRESENT FORM IS A volume of forty-three poems written between 1839 and 1845. They were first published separately, most of them in *La Presse* and in *La Revue des Deux Mondes,* the rest in a variety of journals: *L'Artiste, France musicale, Les Beaux-Arts, La Sylphide, Musée des familles, La France littéraire* and *Revue de Paris.* Both "Le Chasseur" and "Letrilla"—the first and last composed of the collection—are in a sense peripheral: the former appeared in 1839 before Gautier's trip to Spain, while the latter was written after "Adieux à la poésie."[1] Their chronology was first established by Spoelberch de Lovenjoul (*Histoire des œuvres de Théophile Gautier*), who notes that Gautier had intended to publish some of the poems in 1843 in a volume entitled "Poésies espagnoles" (300). It is not known whether Gautier had not produced the requisite number of poems or whether the contract with Désessart was broken for some other reason.

René Jasinski, both in his study *L'"España" de Théophile Gautier* and in his edition of *España,* orders the poems, as did Gautier himself, so as to support the notion of a simple symbolic journey.[2] The transition from romantic gloom to Parnassian sunshine is accordingly paralleled by appropriate changes of setting. Gloomy churches, deserted cemeteries and dark burial vaults yield to azure skies, flowered mountainsides, and sunny gardens. The artist progresses from a gothic melancholy in northern Spain to a sunnier mood in Andalusia. This sequence tends to support Jasinski's view of *España* as "purement romantique . . . parce que l'objet y sert à traduire une âme et que cette âme est pleine encore des images et des frissons de 1830" (Jasinski, *L'España* 46). The antitheses he discerns are emotional rather than esthetic: "autant sa prose a désormais acquis sa robuste opulence, autant sa poésie hésite entre des possibilités contraires: les brumes du nord s'y mêlent curieusement à la blonde lumière méridionale, le frisson à la joie, la méditation à la fantaisie légère" (35). Many of the poems composed between 1840 and 1842 are in fact clearly romantic in inspiration, whereas most of the later poems reveal a renewed preoccupation with form and visual effect.

It was Jasinski's notion of Gautier's journey as having effected a kind of poetic "cure," a notion more simplistic than incorrect, that doubtless encouraged the dismissive responses to *España* it has received for more than sixty years. From 1929, the year that Jasinski's study appeared, to the late 1950s, when critics began to reexamine a number of Gautier's works, *España* was virtually ignored. Jasinski observes of it that "Avec les années elle n'a pas recouvré sa place: l'éclat du *Voyage (en Espagne)* en a fait pâlir la fine couleur, de même que comme recueil poétique, elle perdait un peu de son relief entre la *Comédie de la Mort* et les *Emaux et Camées*" (44). As we have seen, the poet's more sympathetic critics generally discern in it no added dimension, while his detractors fasten upon the romantic poems as derivative or dismiss the later poems—as they would *Emaux et Camées*—as trivial.[3] There is some truth in these judgments: a number of *España*'s poems replicate the *microcosmes* of Gautier's early poetry that would reappear in *Emaux et Camées*. These poems attest to constants in Gautier's art that would seem to belie its evolutionary character; only the landscape has changed. At the same time, Gautier was undeniably under the spell of other romantics during the 1830s, and many of *España*'s darker poems echo Hugo's somber voice. It is unquestionable that the volume chronicles Gautier's relinquishing of the romantic grand manner, and the longer and looser forms congenial to its expression, in favor of a muted lyricism and more condensed forms.

Yet the transition was neither simple nor smooth, and there are those of *España*'s poems that document Gautier's discontent with the romantic mode that have not been recognized as such, in part because the transition itself has not been considered remarkable, but primarily because the poems have not been considered according to their order of composition. The evolution of a thing is its development in time. It follows that the evolution of Gautier's poetics cannot be determined unless his poems are considered as consecutive efforts, especially since they were five years in the writing and only minimally the products of local inspiration. Moreover, the fact that Gautier's composition of the individual poems did not always parallel the sequence of episodes that inspired them complicates the long-held topographical view of *España*'s transitional nature. Even Jasinski, who describes the work categorically as "purement romantique," detects something hesitant about the poems:

> *España*, œuvre de transition, étape incertaine entre la *Comédie de la mort* et les *Emaux et Camées*, révèle plus de souplesse que d'originalité créatrice, et la diversité de modèles trahit moins encore la défaillance de l'inspiration qu'une exécution laborieuse et une poétique indécise. (Jasinski, *L'España* 35)

Gautier's retrospective ordering of his poems imparts a superficial and therefore misleading unity to the volume. It is true that Gautier traveled through "Gothic" Spain before visiting Andalusia, and that he was invigorated by what he saw in southern Spain. His *Voyage en Espagne* testifies abundantly to the galvanizing effects of the perspective he had acquired by the end of his journey. But this perspective helped the prose writer more than it did the poet.[4] Moreover, Gautier had written only a fraction of the poems of *España* before returning home to France, by which time little had been resolved. The evidence of Gautier's indecision, taken from both the poems themselves and from other sources, is unequivocal. Though the dilemma that inspired them is studiedly veiled, it is the subject of a small fraction of *España*'s poems. The year 1842 in particular—two years after his Andalusian experience—emerges as a year of crisis. In this year, which marked his definitive farewell to the romantic model, Gautier wrote no more than three poems. The poet's experience as narrated in one of these, "In Deserto," would be crucial. Finally, Gautier's trip to Spain, long contemplated in the poems of 1838 as a beneficial exile, was decisive but not immediately so. The path Gautier as poet would follow in 1843 and 1844 was an uncertain one; it would lead him between the Parnassians and the Symbolists, and in some respects away from poetry.

The Dilemma

In its simplest form, Gautier's dilemma was how to reconcile his romantic heritage with the rigorous esthetic he professed. He was slow to free himself from the romantic models typified in the poetry of Vigny, Musset, and especially Hugo. His democratic sympathies, especially the impulse to speak to all men, encouraged an expanded verse form whereas his sculptor's instincts demanded compression. As noted earlier, the prototype of *Emaux et Camées*—the *microcosme*—emerges in his earliest efforts, but it alternates with longer meditative poems in which romantic cliché often predominates: the bright cameos stand alongside lengthy expressions of a conventionally romantic melancholy and gloom. In addition, there is the example of the spirited and parodic *Albertus,* which belongs to neither category. What distinguishes *España* from Gautier's earlier and later efforts and from those of his romantic confrères are a handful of poems in which the poet reconciles the three modes in shorter poems. As sequential compositions, these poems constitute a dialectic that would lead to his rejection of the broader romantic forms and confirm the poetics of *Emaux et Camées.*

Throughout *España* there are in fact two kinds of argumentation, the one concerned with substance, the other with form. In the first, minerals, especially precious stones, are proposed as an indestructible medium. The ephemeral world is transformed, fixed, made solid and durable. In "Les Yeux bleus de la montagne," for example, lakes are "purs comme des cristaux, bleus comme des turquoises"; in "Sainte Casilde" drops of blood are "rubis" (*PC* 2, 259); in "La petite fleur rose" there is "l'eau diamantée" (269). But minerals exist in other forms whose connotations are ambivalent. As an intractable element—the metaphor for a poetic absolute—the larger rocks that must be scaled also discourage and intimidate. L'Escurial is "posé comme un défi" . . . an "éléphant monstrueux . . . / Débauche de granit . . ." (276). This stone can be repressive, even paralyzing.[5] The threat had been expressed by Théodore in *Mademoiselle de Maupin*: "Le rêve est devenu un cauchemar, et le chimère un succube; —le monde de l'âme a fermé ses portes d'ivoire devant moi: . . . j'ai des songes de pierre; tout se condense et se durcit autour de moi . . . la matière me presse, m'envahit et m'écrase . . . "(*MM* 198-99).

The other dialectic opposes the discursive and loosely structured poem to one of greater density and prosodic ingenuity. Poems in the first category tend to imitate the romantic epic; those in the latter are often adaptations of Spanish verse forms. The longer and loosely structured poems are generalizations about the artist's plight and the immortality of art. They are usually composed of alexandrines, these characterized by broad rhythmic units and an absence of internal rhyme. Examples of these are "L'Horloge," "A la Bidassoa," "Consolation," "En Passant à Vergara," and "Saint Christophe d'Ecija." The poems that avoid philosophical statement are prosodically more complex. They are characterized by a variety of stanzaic patterns and by a shorter line. This condensed form compels a shorter rhythmic unit and is distinguished by greater richness of rhyme, both end and internal. These poems generally focus upon experiences of lesser moment, upon fleeting glimpses of beauty or the vicissitudes of love. Examples of these would be "Séguidille," "J'ai dans mon cœur," "La Lune," "Letrilla," and "J'ai laissé sur mon sein de neige..."

In certain poems, however—the more complex of Gautier's mineral visions—the two dialectics fuse. The mineral analogue begins to merge with the abstract notion of a "sculpted" poetic form to become what Gautier himself refered to as *"ce bloc de la phrase."*[6] These poems are of varying length and stanzaic pattern, and with a few exceptions, they combine the modes Gautier had earlier essayed separately. They are at once lapidary, ironic, and lyric, and though the argument is advanced in most cases without direct, and often without implied, correlation to the speaker, they reveal a poet both critical and at times self-critical.[7] An ambitious sculptural ideal—the poem's setting is usually mineral, often stony or mountainous—continues to be proposed, but the would-be romantic poet is found wanting, and his weaknesses demonstrated in the diction and shape of the poem. This expression of inadequacy often depends, then, upon a paradoxically "flawed" form that leads the poet to reassess his talent and to redefine his art. In *España,* Gautier eventually abandons the broad vistas and the grand manner of the romantics. In his retreat from the mountain, he scales it down, reducing the mineral block to fragments and miniaturizing them. The last poem expressive of Gautier's "mineral" dilemma, "In Deserto," also resolves it. Gautier's preoccupation with form, with "difficulté vaincue," would ultimately prevail over his desire to reach all men; the poet of *Emaux et Camées* would address a smaller audience.

Chapter IV

The Poems of 1840

GAUTIER COMPLETED THE *FEUILLETONS* that would correspond to the first nine chapters of *Voyage en Espagne* during 1840; these chapters take the travelers from Paris to Madrid via Burgos. Gautier's dark mood dominates the early stages of his journey, particularly in his sensitivity to the gothic and macabre aspects of the country between Paris and Vergara. The morbid ambiance of "La Thébaïde" and *La Comédie de la mort* prevails, and in Burgos (*VE* chapter 4) he is more depressed than elated by the cathedral. Overcome by a sense of futility, he writes:

> Un profond sentiment de tristesse me serre le cœur lorsque je visite un de ces prodigieux édifices des temps passés; il me prend un découragement immense, et je n'aspire plus qu'à me retirer dans un coin, à me mettre une pierre sous la tête, pour attendre, dans l'immobilité de la contemplation, la mort, cette immobilité absolue. A quoi bon travailler? à quoi bon se remuer? L'effort humain le plus violent n'arrivera jamais au-delà. . . . Quand je pense que j'ai usé la meilleure portion de ma vie à rimer dix ou douze mille vers, à écrire six ou sept pauvres volumes in-8 et trois ou quatre cents mauvais articles de journaux, et que je me trouve fatigué, j'ai honte de moi-même et de mon époque, où il faut tant d'efforts pour produire si peu de chose.

> Qu'est-ce qu'une mince feuille de papier à côté d'une montagne de granit? (*VE* 39)

His resignation is apparent in his appreciation of the cathedral, close to one-third of which is digression. His account of it reads more like a tourist brochure than the *transpositions d'art* for which he is noted; it is clichéd ("Ce portail . . . fleuri comme une dentelle," "Cette épopée de pierre") and sprinkled with empty superlatives ("inouï," "incomparable," "incroyable," "inconcevable"), and numerous sentences begin with "Ce sont" or "Ce ne sont que" followed by the details of a wall carving or a choir. These pages are more inventory than evocation, and they lack his usual verve and confidence.

In Madrid, Gautier's *optique* points to his recurrent nihilism. At a bullfight a gored and dying horse prompts him to equate art and death: "sa tête, si noblement et si purement charpentée, modelée et frappée de méplats par le doigt terrible du néant, semble avoir été habitée par une pensée humaine" (*VE* 82). His continued sense of futility is reinforced by memories of Goya. In his transposition of a plate from Goya's *Caprichos, Y aun no se van,* (chapter 8) in which the artist depicts death as the descending slab of a tomb, he writes: "L'expression de désespoir qui se peint sur toutes ces physionomies cadavéreuses, dans ces orbites sans yeux, qui voient que leur labeur a été inutile, est vraiment tragique; c'est le plus triste symbole de l'impuissance laborieuse, la plus sombre poésie et la plus amère dérision que l'on ait jamais faites à propos des morts" (*VE* 121).[1] In these early stages the Escorial looms as the epitome of the oppressive and paralyzing mineral structure: "il vous entoure, il vous enlace et vous étouffe; vous vous sentez pris comme dans les tentacules d'un gigantesque polype de granit" (*VE* 130). These feelings were of long standing, and they are echoed in poems like "L'Escurial" and "J'étais monté plus haut . . ." The sculpted artifact as a metaphor for verbal art had ambivalent implications for the prose writer as well as the poet. He was obsessed with its grandeur and immutability, yet it was precisely these attributes that stifled his exuberance and sense of play. The narrator's temperament throughout most of *Voyage en Espagne*, however, is jocose: he is the enemy of solemnity, the parodist of the sacrosanct, and the apologist for variety and change. His high-spirited account of the carriage ride from Burgos to Madrid, for example, is pure hyberbole, a celebration of movement—of *déplacement*—and sound.[2] But some months would pass before those attributes were integrated to his mineral ideal in *Voyage en Espagne*. Whatever its form, the *bloc minéral* would remain central to Gautier's work, but it cast its darkest shadows from 1840 to 1842.

Gautier wrote seven poems after his departure from Paris in May of 1840, five of which he completed before his return to France from Spain in September of that year. Most of them draw heavily upon the Spanish landscape and perpetuate the emotional extremes characteristic of Gautier's early poetry. "Le Pin des Landes," and "A la Bidassoa," express a generalized melancholy common to the early romantics. The slashed pine in the first is the suffering poet. "A la Bidassoa," the only poem in *España* inspired by the civil war, describes a harvest of bullets rather than wheat; and "l'Escurial" depicts a monument to death. This gloom is attended by breadth of line and rhythmic phrasing, particularly in the narrative poem "A la Bidassoa," and by commonplace romantic images. Phrases like "L'homme, avare bourreau de la création," "tronc douloureux," "divines larmes d'or," "Hélas! ce que Dieu fait, les hommes le défont!" are typical of the effusions to which the romantics were given and which were still congenial to Gautier at the time.

The darkness of these poems is relieved by "Les Yeux bleus de la montagne" and "La Petite fleur rose," these romantic too in subject: the divinity of art. The first, "Les Yeux bleus de la montagne," is composed of two stanzas, each ending with a hemistiche. It is one of many poems in which altitude and hardness are equated with excellence, and in the figure of "Dieu, l'ouvrier jaloux," Gautier touches on the issue of effort, which will become a major preoccupation in 1842. The six-syllable quatrains and the predominance of nouns in the singular of "La Petite fleur rose" recall the focus and concentration of Gautier's *microcosmes*. From the mountain's unquarried "flancs de granit" and from remoter prominences, the poet sculpts a slim vertical column offering a privileged view of a landscape animated by *précieux* touches like "l'hiver pâle assiège / Les pics" and "l'eau diamantée / . . . / D'un caillou tourmentée."[3] Such efforts evidence the constants of Gautier's poetic art, in particular compression and attention to visual effect, though their lyricism is facile and not yet exclusively a function of form. "L'Escurial" is also syntactically tighter than most of the other poems of this year and deserves comment. Despite the monument's sinister appearance in *Voyage en Espagne,* Gautier's evocation of it here is playful:

> Posé comme un défi tout près d'une montagne,
> L'on aperçoit de loin dans la morne compagne
> Le sombre Escurial, à trois cents pieds du sol,
> Soulevant sur le coin de son épaule énorme,
> Eléphant monstrueux, la coupole difforme,
> Débauche de granit du Tibère espagnol.
>
> Jamais vieux Pharaon, au flanc d'un mont d'Egypte,
> Ne fit pour sa momie une plus noire crypte;
> Jamais Sphinx au désert n'a gardé plus d'ennui;
> La cigogne s'endort au bout des cheminées;
> Partout l'herbe verdit les cours abandonnées;
> Moines, prêtres, soldats, courtisans, tout a fui!
>
> Et tout semblerait mort, si du bord des corniches,
> Des mains des rois sculptés, des frontons et des niches,
> Avec leurs cris charmants et leur folle gaîté,
> Il ne s'envolait pas des essaims d'hirondelles,
> Qui, pour le réveiller, agacent à coups d'ailes
> Le géant assoupi qui rêve éternité!... (*PC* 2, 276).

Built by Juan de Herrera for Philip II, l'Escorial was to function as palace, monastery, library, and tomb. Where in *Voyage en Espagne* Gautier had described it as menacing, here he laughs at the artless colossus: the imposing palace in this evocation is more zoo than royal residence. Allusions to Pharoahs, Sphinxes, the armies of church and state, and the unyielding "granit du Tibère espagnol" erect a solemn and forbidding structure,[4] but the images of the sleeping elephant and pecking swallows prevail. The same mélange of gothic and comic that characterizes *Albertus* recurs in several of the later poems of *España*.

Only two poems of this year, "Le Poète et la foule" and "J'étais monté plus haut . . ." can be said to bear more closely on Gautier's dilemma. Both were written two months after Gautier's return to Paris, when the euphoria of his Spanish experience would have subsided. "Le Poète et la foule," though superficially naive, is the most complex of the poems of 1840, and the one that most fully articulates Gautier's reservations at this stage. This poem of four quatrains, an oblique defense of art for art's sake, caricaturizes romantic pretention. It is composed of two dialogues, the first between mountain and plain, the second between the poet and "la foule."

> La plaine un jour disait à la montagne oisive:
> —Rien ne vient sur ton front des vents toujours battu!
> Au poète, courbé sur sa lyre pensive,
> La foule aussi disait: —Rêveur, à quoi sers-tu?
>
> La montagne en courroux répondit à la plaine:
> —C'est moi qui fais germer les moissons sur ton sol;
> Du midi dévorant je tempère l'haleine;
> J'arrête dans les cieux les nuages au vol!
>
> Je pétris de mes doigts la neige en avalanches;
> Dans mon creuset je fonds les cristaux des glaciers,
> Et je verse, du bout de mes mamelles blanches,

En longs filets d'argent, les fleuves nourriciers.

Le poète, à son tour, répondit à la foule:
—Laissez mon pâle front s'appuyer sur ma main.
N'ai-je pas de mon flanc, d'où mon âme s'écoule,
Fait jaillir une source où boit le genre humain? (*PC* 2, 292)

In the first stanza, poet and mountain are equated and two lines assigned to each. The central quatrains, however, are devoted to the mountain's defense of itself, which has the effect of eclipsing the speaker of the last quatrain and dramatizing his effeteness. The poem's figuration supports such a reading, suggesting that for Gautier even utility was preferable to self-indulgence in poetry. The mountain, an immobile yet dynamic colossus, is depicted as confident; the poet as uncertain. Gautier's revised third line, "courbé sur sa lyre pensive," also supports this characterization. (The original, "Au poète penché sur sa lyre pensive," would have described a poet less stooped.[5]) The mountain here is cast as a benevolent Zeus; the romantic poet as a whining Prometheus. Finally, in his evocation of the "montagne oisive," Gautier points to the galling irony of achievement realized without effort, an irony that would increasingly frustrate his resolve.

"J'étais monté plus haut . . ."—the ellipsis is significant, indicating as it does something abandoned—is the first poem in which the monolith intimidates. Here the poet retreats before the challenge of amorphous rock:

J'étais monté plus haut que l'aigle et le nuage;
Sous mes pieds s'étendait un vaste paysage,
Cerclé d'un double azur par le ciel et la mer;
Et les crânes pelés des montagnes géantes
En foule jaillissaient des profondeurs béantes,
Comme de blancs écueils sortant du gouffre amer.

C'était un vaste amas d'éboulements énormes,

> Des rochers grimaçant dans des poses difformes,
> Des pics dont l'œil à peine embrasse la hauteur,
> Et, la neige faisant une écume à leur crête,
> On eût dit une mer prise un jour de tempête,
> Un chaos attendant le mot du Créateur.
>
> Là dorment les débris des races disparues,
> Le vieux monde noyé sous les ondes accrues,
> Le Béhémot biblique et le Léviathan.
> Chaque mont de la chaîne, immense cimetière,
> Cache un corps monstrueux dans son ventre de pierre,
> Et ses blocs de granit sont des os de Titan! (*PC* 2, 289)

This poem, particularly its grandiose perspectives and its evocation of a grotesquely anthropomorphized nature, owes much to romantic convention. It contemplates a Hugolian landscape, but where Hugo would expand, Gautier condenses. The first stanza is full of movement, but in the second a preponderance of substantives slows it, freezing it into the immobility of the last stanza. This concentration of effect, more typical of his mature poetry in which thought is subordinated to sensation, here serves to dramatize the poet's self-doubts. The tensions between the static and dynamic elements of the poem betray a mounting anxiety, and the poet's changing mood and perspective prompt his flight from this mineral threat, a retreat borne out by the absence of the personal pronoun after the first stanza—the mountain climber disappears behind "l'œil" and "l'on"—and the menacing aspect of the imagined spectacle in the last stanza. Prometheus, then, has abandoned his post. The changed size and appearance of the characters in his tableau suggest an altered perception: the anthropomorphized mountains—the "bald men"—of the first stanza have become the monsters of the last.

The monolith in "J'étais monté plus haut . . . ," recalls the Escorial of *Voyage en Espagne,* rather than the Escorial of "L'Escurial," a wittier and more confident poem. Both "Le Poète et la foule" and "J'étais monté plus haut . . ." are self-conscious, self-critical as well as critical. In "Le Poète et la foule," the effete romantic—though he ministers to spiritual need—is outdone by a better poet, the versatile and productive mountain. In "J'étais monté plus haut . . ." the poet is timid and unable to exploit his resources, and there is in addition here a feeling of repression and fear of burial. In both instances stone—the mountain—is dramatized as an intimidating force. The poems of the year to come would expose other weaknesses in the romantic poet.

Chapter V
The Poems of 1841

THE TWO *FEUILLETONS* GAUTIER WROTE in 1841 were destined for the *Revue de Paris*. The first would become chapter 10 of *Voyage en Espagne* and describes his visit to Toledo. The second, which corresponds to the first twenty-five pages of chapter 11 in the travel book, chronicles the travelers' return to Madrid and their journey into southern Spain as far as Jaen. In Toledo Gautier discovered the mixed blessings of exile: he had escaped from the modernity of Madrid, which reminded him too much of the progress he deplored in his own culture, but the old city also deepened his sense of isolation. At one point, looking over a wall atop the Alcazar, he notes,

> . . . il me prenait des doutes sur ma propre identité, je me sentais si absent de moi-même, transporté si loin de ma sphère, que tout cela me paraissait une hallucination, un rêve étrange dont j'allais me réveiller en sursaut au son aigre et chevrotant de quelque musique de vaudeville sur le rebord d'une loge du théâtre . . . malgré la magnificence du spectacle, je me sentais l'âme envahie par une tristesse incommensurable, et pourtant j'accomplissais le rêve de toute ma vie, je touchais du doigt un de mes désirs les plus ardemment caressés. (*VE* 145)

One can view the experience as simple homesickness, but it is also possible to see in it a turning point, the separation hoped for in

"Thébaïde," and a diminution of the poet's morbid sensibilities.[1] In any event, in Toledo Gautier's transpositions begin increasingly to bear the stamp of his comic genius.

His description of the Toledo cathedral, like that of the cathedral in Burgos, is in many respects what one would expect to find in a guide. But there is in these pages an effort towards synthesis along with a shift in tone, and there are fewer digressions. His account begins, for example, with a mildly irreverent retelling of the church's history prefaced by the legend of the Virgin of Toledo, the effect of which is to surround the structure with an aura of playful fantasy. There is also at times a vibrancy and animation absent from earlier descriptions of architecture, as in

> . . . toute cette architecture, qui monte jusqu'à la voûte et qui fait le tour du sanctuaire, est peinte et dorée avec une richesse inimaginable. Les tons fauves et chauds de l'antique dorure font ressortir splendidement les filets et les paillettes de lumière accrochés au passage par les nervures et les saillies des ornements, et produisent des effets admirables de la plus grande opulence pittoresque. (*VE* 150)

Gautier endows the *retablo* with a muscled—one might even say acrobatic—presence (in "monte," "fait le tour" and "accrochés"), having earlier covered it with skin "d'une teinte rousse, d'une couleur rôtie grillée, d'un épiderme hâlé comme celui d'un pèlerin de Palestine" (*VE* 149). Here Gautier perceives of the cathedral as theater: "La musique y est meilleure qu'au théâtre, et la pompe du spectacle n'a pas de rival. C'est le point central, le lieu attrayant, comme l'Opéra à Paris" (*VE* 155).[2]

The fourteen poems of 1841, inspired by Spanish artifacts as well as by Spanish landscapes, convey much of the Spanish character and sensibility. A number of them—"J'ai dans mon cœur," "Au bord de la mer" and "Sérénade"—like those of the preceding year, are imitations of Spanish verse forms. Though virtuoso pieces, they are primarily exercises in adaptation. Three others are *transpositions d'art:* "Saint-Christophe d'Ecija," "La Vierge de Tolède" and "Un Tableau de Valdès Léal."[3] The first two narrate the legends that inspired the sculpture. The third is a denunciation of Spanish realism, one of several in the volume. Most of these poems reveal little of the poet. The transpositions are extended stichic meditations, or diatribes, typical of early romanticism. "Saint-Christophe d'Ecija" echoes "J'étais monté plus haut . . ." in its appreciation of titanic strength, but the characterization is essentially Hugolian and reveals the continued influence of Gautier's mentors and none of his reservations. The same is true of "La Vierge de Tolède," a poeticized legend that suffers from prosiness as well as from superfluous interjection.

The poet's happier moods are again captured in the *précieux* poems and his recurrent pessimism elaborated in the longer ones. Most of these are disquisitions upon threats to art and life. "En Passant à Vergara" is a heavily ironic poem in the romantic tradition that juxtaposes the vibrancy of a young Spanish servant to the macabre visions inspired by a passing funeral procession. "L'Horloge" creates a similar effect through its evocation of death in the midst of life. "Consolation," like earlier efforts, equates art with mountain heights and enjoins poets to persevere, though it too betrays defensiveness ("Ne sois pas étonné si la foule, ô poète, / Dédaigne de gravir ton œuvre jusqu'au faîte;" [*PC* 2, 290]).

A number of poems are, again, introspective and self-conscious, and they bring the poet to the eve of his crisis. One of these, the poem "Départ," which Gautier placed at the beginning of the collection, illuminates the poet's disposition and his preoccupations at this juncture. It was published in September of 1841, after he had already composed eleven of *España*'s poems. Rambling and discursive—it is the longest poem of the collection—"Départ" recapitulates the apprehensions of *La Comédie de la mort* and "Thébaïde." As a preface to the volume, the poem prepares the reader for departure, making much of the desire for renewal common to many disillusioned and restless romantics.[4] As an invitation to travel, however, it is not very encouraging. Though hopeful at the outset, by the end the poet has lost his enthusiasm; only a dog and a spider await his return; his absence has gone unnoticed.[5] He intended it as a preface to the whole collection of poems in *España*, but "Départ" more appropriately introduces the poems of 1841 that followed its composition by virtue of the poet's *désarroi*—Jasinski remarks of it that "la composition flotte un peu" (Jasinski *L'España* 58). In the second section, in which ennui dampens the enthusiasm of the traveler's earlier "rêves palpitants" (*PC* 2, 252), the stony mountain provides a now familiar decor as the poet repeats the wish expressed in "Thébaïde"[6]:

> Et sur l'âpre rocher où descend le vautour
> Je me rongeais le foie en attendant le jour.
> Je sentais le désir d'être absent de moi-même;
> Loin de ceux que je hais et loin de ceux que j'aime,
> Sur une terre vierge et sous un ciel nouveau,
> Je voulais écouter mon cœur et mon cerveau,
> Et savoir, fatigué de stériles études,
> Quels baumes contenait l'urne des solitudes. (*PC* 2, 252)

These lines recall the enfeebled Prometheus of "Le Poète et la foule." Here again the poet's depiction of him is unconventional. It is critical of the self-absorbed poet ("Je me rongeais le foie"), pointing to Baudelaire and to others who looked inward to find nemeses as threatening to art as death or critical rejection. "Départ" signals an excursion into sterility that would be poetically chronicled,[7] particularly in "Dans la Sierra."

The ruined state in which the civil war had left many Spanish monasteries doubtless appealed to Gautier's morbid sensibilities. The bleak setting of "La Fontaine du cimetière," which depicts an abandoned *Chartreuse,* is one of the more self-critical of the poems of *España*. It serves to objectify a paralysis consequent upon blindness:

> A la morne Chartreuse, entre des murs de pierre,
> En place de jardin l'on voit un cimetière,
> Un cimetière nu comme un sillon fauché,
> Sans croix, sans monument, sans tertre qui se hausse:
> L'oubli couvre le nom, l'herbe couvre la fosse;
> La mère ignorerait où son fils est couché.
>
> Les végétations maladives du cloître
> Seules sur ce terrain peuvent germer et croître,
> Dans l'humidité froide à l'ombre des longs murs;
> Des morts abandonnés douces consolatrices,
> Les fleurs n'oseraient pas incliner leurs calices
> Sur le vague tombeau de ces dormeurs obscurs.
>
> Au milieu, deux cyprès à la noire verdure
> Profilent tristement leur silhouette dure,
> Longs soupirs de feuillage élancés vers les cieux,
> Pendant que du bassin d'une avare fontaine
> Tombe en frange effilé une nappe incertaine,
> Comme des pleurs furtifs qui débordent des yeux.
>
> Par les saints ossements des vieux moines filtrée,
> L'eau coule à flots si clairs dans la vasque éplorée,
> Que pour en boire un peu je m'approchai du bord . . .
> Dans le cristal glacé quand je trempai ma lèvre,
> Je me sentis saisi par un frisson de fièvre:
> Cette eau de diamant avait un goût de mort! (*PC* 2, 261)

In this poem, description serves the expression of apprehension and impotence. Unlike the gothic settings of *Albertus* and *La Comédie de la mort,* with their richly decadent appointments, the graveyard of this Carthusian monastery offers little to the eye. There are no grave markers, and nothing is given definition or presence. Negation and a thematics of hollowness point to a fear of oblivion, and the diction of the poem suggests increasing blindness. This poverty of vision is intensified by the juxtaposition of what might be to what is, and by an insistence upon what is missing, a technique Gautier would use to greater effect in "In Deserto." The problem of seeing little is exacerbated by the inability to see clearly. Objects in the first two stanzas are perceived distinctly, yet from line fourteen onward their outlines become blurred, as in "vague tombeau" and "dormeurs obscurs." To the clearly defined figures of the cypresses, which themselves dissolve into "longs soupirs de feuillage," are opposed the "frange effilé" of a "nappe incertaine," along with "pleurs furtifs." The dynamics of the poem—like those of "J'étais monté plus haut . . ."—compound this inability to focus with paralysis. Every hint of life and creation is stifled and repressed. In the second stanza, the vertical movement implied in "germer" and "croître," is countered by absent flowers "qui n'oseraient pas incliner leurs calices." In the third stanza again "arise" two cypresses, whose upward thrust is similarly qualified by the static "profilent" and the falling water and tears. The quasi-mineral imagery in this poem, then—the deserted cemetery, the immobile cypresses, the diamond-like water—is as much an expression of *impuissance* as it is of fear of death.[8]

"Dans la Sierra," like "J'étais monté plus haut . . . ," also describes difficulties with vision. It has often been anthologized, and editors have usually praised it as an exemplary defense of *l'art pour l'art*. The poet is likened to the *alpiniste* and the poem to the mountain peak he must scale. As do several of the poems of 1840 it deifies beauty, equating art with altitude, but like others of that year it also depicts the mountain as formidable and inaccessible not only to ordinary men but also to the poet. The "flaws" in this poem—its clichés and its superfluous comment—serve a poetic end, again revealing the poet as ineffectual:

J'aime d'un fol amour les monts fiers et sublimes!
Les plantes n'osent pas poser leurs pieds frileux
Sur le linceul d'argent qui recouvre leurs cimes;
Le soc s'émousserait à leurs pics anguleux.

Ni vigne aux bras lascifs, ni blés dorés, ni seigles;
Rien qui rappelle l'homme et le travail maudit.
Dans leur air libre et pur nagent des essaims d'aigles,
Et l'écho du rocher siffle l'air du bandit.

Ils ne rapportent rien et ne sont pas utiles;
Ils n'ont que leur beauté, je le sais, c'est bien peu;
Mais, moi, je les préfère aux champs gras et fertiles,
Qui sont si loin du ciel qu'on n'y voit jamais Dieu! (*PC* 2, 291)

There is a downward progression in the poem: the poet's initial exhilaration is superseded by a defensiveness that builds to the deprecation of the last quatrain. This decline is initially a function of sensory perspective. At the outset the poet revels in the grandeur of the summit, yet in the second quatrain, having lowered his gaze, he hears only the echo of the song rather than the song itself. In the final quatrain, the poet no longer sees the mountaintop, and his poem ends in negation rather than affirmation. This literal retreat parallels the development of other difficulties as the poem becomes less a poem. In the first quatrain the poet's vision, which opposes weakness to strength, is richly figured. Especially in line two, rhythm, assonance, and alliteration help to suggest fragility whereas the gutterals in line four replicate the clash of blade with stone.[9] The poet of the central quatrain, however, is less inventive: in line five the provocative "vigne aux bras lascifs" yields to the clichés "blés dorés" and "travail maudit." This apoetic tendency is reinforced by the increased prosaism and unsettling staccato rhythms of the last quatrain. Here the poet virtually abandons his poem: the lyric élan of the first quatrain has degenerated into sarcasm. As in the "mountain" poems of 1840, the poet retreats or is otherwise diminished.

The last of the self-critical poems of this year, "Le Roi solitaire," is also the most enigmatic. In this poem inspired by Philip II, a sovereign of monastic temperament who for years cloistered himself in his Escorial, the subject of Gautier's earlier poem by that name, the poet addresses his doubts in a broader context but in a more restrictive form. Here, as in "Dans la Sierra," stone plays a double role: it is both tower and prison:

> Je vis cloîtré dans mon âme profonde,
> Sans rien d'humain, sans amour, sans amis,
> Seul comme un dieu, n'ayant d'égaux au monde
> Que mes aïeux sous la tombe endormis!
> Hélas! grandeur veut dire solitude.
> Comme une idole au geste surhumain,
> Je reste là, gardant mon attitude,
> La pourpre au dos, le monde dans la main.
>
> Comme Jésus, j'ai le cercle d'épines;
> Les rayons d'or du nimbe sidéral
> Percent ma peau comme des javelines,
> Et sur mon front perle mon sang royal.
> Le bec pointu du vautour héraldique
> Fouille mon flanc en proie aux noirs soucis:
> Sur son rocher, le Prométhée antique
> N'était qu'un roi sur son fauteuil assis.
>
> De mon olympe entouré de mystère,
> Je n'entends rien que la voix des flatteurs;
> C'est le seul bruit qui des bruits de la terre
> Puisse arriver à de telles hauteurs;
> Et si parfois mon peuple, qu'on outrage,
> En gémissant entre-choque ses fers:
> —Sire! dormez, me dit-on, c'est l'orage;
> Les cieux bientôt vont devenir plus clairs.

> Je puis tout faire, et je n'ai plus d'envie.
> Ah! si j'avais seulement un désir!
> Si je sentais la chaleur de la vie!
> Si je pouvais partager un plaisir!
> Mais le soleil va toujours sans cortège;
> Les plus hauts monts sont aussi les plus froids;
> Et nul été ne peut fondre la neige
> Sur les sierras et dans le cœur des rois! (*PC* 2, 277-78)

In this poem the poet-king rationalizes his failures. In four stanzas he walls himself in, claustrating himself with his own rhetoric. His disingenuousness is suggested by his shifting tone and by the circularity of his arguments, this echoed in images such as "Je vis cloîtré," "j'ai le cercle d'épines," "nimbe sidéral." He is by turns pitiable and pretentious, now Spanish monarch, now Jesus, now Prometheus, as complaint alternates with posturing. The pompous "mon âme profonde," "mon olympe," and "Prométhée . . . sur son fauteuil assis" further subvert the pathos of his appeal, and there is added irony in Gautier's use of the decasyllable, a measure common to both epic and satire.[10] Like Mallarmé, who would become frozen in his "exil inutil," the poet of "Le Roi solitaire" is alone responsible for his plight: he has cemented himself into immobility. The problem of communication, or perhaps better, of audience, would also inspire the poet of "In Deserto." The experience of this poem, then, is decidedly equivocal: it is both ironic—a criticism of the romantic ambition to speak to all men—and lyric, expressing the pain of the poet who can speak to no one.

With the possible exception of "La Fontaine du cimetière," in which the gothic element is understated and deftly handled, these poems reveal Gautier's increasing dissatisfaction with the romantic mode if not with himself. Their diction is still romantic, but with the exception of "Départ," they are briefer and more condensed than the lyric poems of 1840, and the last of them, "Le Roi solitaire," verges on parody. The retreat described in "Dans la Sierra" and the rationalized *paresse* of "Le Roi solitaire" suggest the ineffectual romantic, who in the first instance moralizes and in the second whines.[11] In the coming year the question of mode and audience would again be raised in mineral form; in a single poem the mountain would crumble, its remains testifying both to loss and gain.

Chapter VI

The Poems of 1842

THE YEAR 1842 APPEARS TO have been generally bleak for Gautier. It began unpromisingly enough. On January 17, Gautier's work as secretary to the commission charged with recommending a fitting memorial to Napoléon led to his being named Chevalier de la Légion d'Honneur, a distinction his colleagues—and he himself no doubt—felt should have been awarded him for his literary accomplishments.[1] He continued to review theatrical performances and to produce art and literary criticism at his normal rate, but he was a rather perfunctory correspondent during this year. His letters are for the most part brief and show little evidence of his usual outspokenness and wit.[2] Gautier composed two *feuilletons* for *La Revue des Deux-Mondes* in 1842. These became the end of chapter 11, and chapters 12-14 in *Voyage en Espagne,* and they take the reader through Granada, Málaga, Córdoba, and Seville. Andalusia, which had inspired the traveler's hopes, left him disillusioned. In *Voyage en Espagne* he concedes the superiority of Moorish sculptural design but complains of its lack of dynamism and originality. In the Alhambra he reserves his more inventive accounts of his visit for the garden—the Generalife.[3] In Málaga, Gautier is all praise for Spanish drama of the Golden Age, of which he observes: "Les Espagnols, bien avant Shakspeare, ont inventé le drame; leur théâtre est romantique dans toute l'acception du mot" (*VE* 288-89).[4] For the prose writer at least, the experience of southern Spain would be decisive.

In Andalusia Gautier *poète* was also approaching a critical period—late July through mid-August of 1842. During these weeks he was writing the *feuilletons* describing his travels through southern Spain that would become chapter 12 of *Voyage en Espagne*.[5] Two episodes narrated in this chapter bear directly upon these weeks and help to clarify the poet's state of mind at the time. One is the account of a bullfight in Málaga and the other of a play he attended later the same evening. After the performance, he reflects upon the contrast between the overcrowded stadium and the almost empty theater. He asks, "A quoi tient la popularité?" (*VE* 283) and then concludes: "ce n'est pas la faute du peuple, si les théâtres ne sont pas plus attrayants; tant pis pour nous, poètes, si nous nous laissons vaincre par les gladiateurs," having reproached the modern dramatist of lacking "ce qui nous manque à tous, la certitude, un point de départ assuré, un fonds d'idées communes avec le public" (292). There is in this casual indictment of himself and his peers a concession to popular taste that is uncharacteristic of him, a sympathy for the larger public who once flocked to the theater of Shakespeare, and before that, of Lope de Vega. Gautier's preoccupation with his readership and with the form and substance of his art would culminate in "In Deserto," published two weeks later on August 28.

Gautier published only three poems in 1842. The first, "Les Trois Grâces de Grenade," which, like "Séguidille" and "Sérénade," celebrates the beauty of Spanish women, appeared in *La Sylphide* on July 3. The poem is superficially romantic: it combines the exotic imagery of southern Spain with romantic commonplaces: Oriental "nymphes de Jénil" and "péris" alternate with "fins cavaliers," "roses de l'aurore," and "yeux nacrés." Here feminine stereotypes, described successively at increased distances from the poet, dramatize his difficulty in speaking to the women, a difficulty aggravated by his inability to address them in Spanish and his tendency to perceive them as part of the Andalusian landscape.[6] (The poem is in fact as much an evocation of the Alhambra as it is of Spanish beauty.) The poet's reference to Zoraïde and Fatmé, women celebrated in legend and in the Spanish romance, compounds their remoteness, as does his final vision of them as combined, representing an ideal or an essence. A similar difficulty in communicating is the chief source of the poet's distress in the second poem of 1842, "In Deserto." The third poem of that year, "Sainte Casilde," is Gothic in inspiration and evokes the horrors of *la légende noire* (*la leyenda negra*), perpetuated by exaggerated tales of cruelty associated with the Spanish Inquisition.[7]

Both "In Deserto" and "Sainte Casilde" appeared on August 28 in the *Revue de Paris,* two weeks later than the *feuilleton* that describes the theater performance in Málaga and Gautier's subsequent remarks about the vagaries of popular taste.[8] According to Jasinski, "In Deserto" was inspired by a desert near La Guardia in the region of la Mancha. The poem details the geological features of a composite Spanish wilderness in its evocation of an aridity exceeded only by the poet's.[9] The equation was not new; the *désert du cœur* had served other romantic poets suffering from emotional atrophy, in particular Sainte-Beuve in his *Poésies de Joseph Delorme*.[10] But "In Deserto" is more than an extended cliché, as some critics have maintained. It is the most unequivocal expression of poetic impotence in *España*.

> Les pitons des sierras, les dunes du désert,
> Où ne pousse jamais un seul brin d'herbe vert;
> Les monts aux flancs zébrés de tuf, d'ocre et de marne,
> Et que l'éboulement de jour en jour décharne;
> Le grès plein de micas papillotant aux yeux,
> Le sable sans profit buvant les pleurs des cieux,
> Le rocher renfrogné dans sa barbe de ronce,
> L'ardente solfatare avec la pierre-ponce,
> Sont moins secs et moins morts aux végétations
> Que le roc de mon cœur ne l'est aux passions.
> Le soleil de midi, sur le sommet aride,
> Répand à flots plombés sa lumière livide,

Et rien n'est plus lugubre et désolant à voir
Que ce grand jour frappant sur ce grand désespoir.
Le lézard pâmé bâille, et parmi l'herbe cuite
On entend résonner les vipères en fuite.
Là, point de marguerite au cœur étoilé d'or,
Point de muguet prodigue égrenant son trésor;
Là, point de violette ignorée et charmante,
Dans l'ombre se cachant comme une pâle amante:
Mais la broussaille rousse et le tronc d'arbre mort,
Que le genou du vent comme un arc plie et tord;
Là, pas d'oiseau chanteur, ni d'abeille en voyage,
Pas de ramier plaintif déplorant son veuvage:
Mais bien quelque vautour, quelque aigle montagnard,
Sur le disque enflammé fixant son œil hagard,
Et qui, du haut du pic où son pied prend racine,
Dans l'or fauve du soir durement se dessine.
Tel était le rocher que Moïse, au désert,
Toucha de sa baguette, et dont le flanc ouvert,
Tressaillant tout à coup, fit jaillir en arcade
Sur les lèvres du peuple une fraîche cascade.
Ah! S'il venait à moi, dans mon aridité,
Quelque reine des cœurs, quelque divinité,
Une magicienne, un Moïse femelle,
Traînant dans le désert les peuples après elle,
Qui frappât le rocher de mon cœur endurci,
Comme de l'autre roche, on en verrait aussi
Sortir en jets d'argent étincelantes,
Où viendraient s'abreuver les racines des plantes;
Où les pâtres errants conduiraient leurs troupeaux,
Pour se coucher à l'ombre et prendre le repos;
Où, comme en un vivier, les cigognes fidèles
Plongeraient leurs grands becs et laveraient leurs ailes.

(*PC* 2, 281)

"In Deserto" recalls the romantic poems of 1840 and 1841 that draw upon landscape to intensify pathos, but here the poet's complaint is ambivalent. The poem is, superficially at least, a lover's lament. Its unabashed lyricism is startlingly intense for one of Gautier's reserve, especially when one considers that Gautier's love life seems to have been flourishing at the time. Letters from Carlotta Grisi and especially from Narcisse Odoïle during this period suggest that his affections were requited (*Correspondance* 1, 286-365). "In Deserto" is more than a plea for love or restored sensibility: it is the poet's farewell to the broader forms of romantic poetry. It also raises doubts, latent in some of the poems of 1840, about the possibility of poetry, pointing ahead to similar doubts expressed in the early poetry of Mallarmé.

The poem consists of three sections: the first (lines 1-14) contains the basic simile: my heart is as dry and dead as the desert; the second (lines 15-32) juxtaposes what is to what might be if some miracle were to cause water to flow; in the last section (lines 33-44) the poet yearns for a similar miracle to soften his heart so that others might look to him to be restored. It would seem to be a simple appeal: the poet cries out for someone to soften his hardened heart so that he might love again. Figuratively, the barren womb would be made to conceive and give birth; the poet would be moved to write. Michael Riffaterre has argued that the true significance of "In Deserto" is limited to such a deciphering of the semiotic desert code, and that the mimetic element of the poem serves only to reinforce the code of loneliness. But Riffaterre disregards much of the central section of the poem, and his reading consequently oversimplifies the poet's complaint (Riffaterre 6-12).[11]

The figure "Moïse femelle" in particular encourages a more complex reading of the poem because it underscores the ambiguity of the poet's sexual desire and consequently of his lament. The poet might have described a figure more consistent with his need simply to be awakened by love, one unequivocally female. That the chosen figure is androgynous raises the question of the poet's own sexual identity in the figurative context of the poem. It suggests that the role he seeks to play is more passive than aggressive.[12] The poet of "In Deserto" wants to be awakened and inspired to act. But he also wants to recline and to be struck, or better, penetrated—"Tel était le rocher que Moïse, au désert / Toucha de sa baguette . . ."—which implies a reversal of both sexual and creative roles. Like the contemplative poet of Mauperthuis, he would create magically, effortlessly, since to act—to write—is to destroy. (The forces of sun and wind suggest such destruction, allegorizing the effects of exertion while pointing ahead to Mallarmé. "Flancs zébrés," suggests a lashing, and there are other examples of brutality: "l'éboulement [qui] . . . décharne," "le genou du vent [qui] plie et tord," and "ce grand jour frappant.")

The poet's fruitful indolence is suggested by what is missing—and its expression here in the singular gives it relief, rendering it quasi symbolic—by the sheltered flora and fauna of the poem's central section. This strategy of negation reinforces the lover's characterization of himself as lacking, describing what cannot flourish in his heart of stone, but it also rationalizes the poet's passivity, his preference for the poem realized without effort, the imagined poem.[13] These creatures are enviable: their beauty is their languor. The coy and retiring "muguet égrenant son trésor," the "violette ignorée . . . se cachant," "le ramier plaintif" and "le lézard pâmé" are virtually static yet potent figures. This opposition between action and repose is rhythmically sustained throughout the poem. Violence is conveyed by impulsive rhythms, these a function of recurring initial accents in most of the early hemistiches; rest and passivity are conveyed in the gentler cadences, especially towards the end of the poem where subject—and therefore to some extent accent—follows verb. The absence of stanzaic divisions also helps to sustain the poetic complaint, hastening its progression towards the central and unifying figure of "Moïse femelle." Viewed in this light, Gautier's arid desert does far more than objectify his hardened heart, though it does that too. It becomes a metaphor for the paradoxes of poetic endeavor. The third section of the poem proposes the miraculous solution, reconciling the antitheses of the first two parts in the figure of the wand, the magical pen.[14]

Finally, as is the case with most of Gautier's earlier poems about poetry, the pathos of "In Deserto" is tempered by a parodic impulse. In some respects the poem approaches a burlesquing of epic. The poet's *vox clamans,* absent from the title, is qualified by the very grotesquery of the wished-for female Moses, the androgynous patriarch ("Traînant dans le désert les peuples après elle"—the image does not flatter), and the concluding pastoral vision is disturbed by ungainly birds. These figures, together with the anthropomorphized desert life, complicate the poem's lyricism, pointing ahead to the multitonal poems of 1843 and 1844. The poem also looks ahead to the poet's definitive *rupture* with romanticism in 1850 and his renewed classicism[15] in that the figure "Moïse femelle" hints at Cybele, pagan earth mother and counterpart of the life-giving biblical Moses. (Baudelaire, in his sonnet "Bohémiens en voyage," written during his "période païenne," also merges the two figures in describing the poet's quest: "Cybèle, qui les aime, augmente ses verdures, / Fait couler le rocher et fleurir le désert" [*BOC* 1, 21]).

The desert of "In Deserto" is then a crucible of sorts, the locus of a decision.[16] The poem brings to an end the debate begun with "Le Poète et la foule." It is the last of the self-conscious poems of *España,* an adieu to the Hugolian model of lyric grandeur that in many respects equals that model in resonance and power even as it is rejecting of it. Though it is not altogether clear whether Gautier *would* no longer or *could* no longer follow in the footsteps of the older generation of romantics, in this poem he is poised for the last time between mountain and *microcosme.* Here the resistant mountain finally yields. The stone prominences of the poems of 1840 and 1841 are broken down and transformed into more manageable substances. They are literally pulverized in the first lines of the poem, whose "pitons," "monts," "micas," "rochers" and "solfatares" foreshadow the smaller stones and gems—the octosyllables—of *Emaux et Camées*. Gautier had made peace, albeit an uneasy one, with his poetic heritage. His sensibilities would remain polarized to some extent, and the mineral world would continue to serve the miniaturist and lapidary, but in the service of a more discreet lyricism, not as a vehicle for debate.[17]

Chapter VII

The Poems of 1843

THE *FEUILLETONS* THAT BECAME CHAPTERS 13 and 14 of *Voyage en Espagne* appeared on November 1 in the *Revue des Deux-Mondes*. The first describes Córdoba, the second Seville. There can be no doubt that between Gautier's writing of chapter 12 and his composition of these chapters a change had occurred. The traveler's experience in the cathedral of Seville reveals a different man. His general outlook, as well as his attitude towards his own writing, is positive, and his account of the cathedral of Seville, Spain's largest, represents the joyful climax of his journey. His exuberant evocation of the immense structure, which ironically now crushes and elates ("L'on est écrasé de magnificences" [*VE* 330]), is the culminating *transposition d'art* of *Voyage en Espagne*:

> Les pagodes indoues les plus effrénées et les plus monstrueusement prodigieuses n'approchent pas de la cathédrale de Séville. C'est une montagne creuse, une vallée renversée; Notre-Dame de Paris se promènerait la tête haute dans la nef du milieu, qui est d'une élévation épouvantable; des piliers gros comme des tours, et qui paraissent frêles à faire frémir, s'élancent du sol ou retombent des voûtes comme les stalactites d'une grotte de géants. Les quatre nefs latérales, quoique moins hautes, pourraient abriter des églises avec leur clocher. (*VE* 328)

In this passage, the cathedral is sublime because grotesque. As an unfinished composite of architectural styles, it is a *mélange des contraires* on a large scale. It is a place of worship, but it is also an antic colossus, a mineral circus, a vaudeville in stone. Here Gautier animates it by dislodging inferior geological and architectural features and setting them in motion. The cathedral pillars become leaping acrobats, its naves brooding hens. Even more than in Toledo, the church is seen as spectacle. The separate designs, shapes, contours, and projections—all the fixed concreteness of earlier churches—disappear, yielding to a more free-wheeling celebration of grandeur, to the expression of a "prospect général." His tribute to the cathedral organ, for example, is impressionistic, embracing storms, battlefields, birds, and angels. His response to the single canvas he describes, Murillo's *Vision of Saint Anthony of Padua,* is to its drama and luminosity. Gautier's experience here is, then, an epiphany of sorts. The mineral artifact no longer paralyzes: as the expression of past achievement it is immutable, yet as an uncompleted structure it is perfectible. The presence of a crane atop its unfinished portal is an invitation to sculptor and writer alike, and Gautier emerges from the cathedral galvanized.

One cannot know precisely what occurred between late August and early November to effect such a change—Gautier wrote one monograph, a few reviews and a revision during those months—nor can one with certainty draw too many parallels between the problem as it presented itself for the prose writer and the crisis facing the poet. What is clear in both cases is that the mineral artifact as a symbol of enduring and incomparable art no longer intimidated either one. Though Gautier continued to be haunted by imagined perfection, the mineral world would no longer inform debate as it had been earlier expressed in his prose. The *feuilleton* that would become the last chapter of *Voyage en Espagne,* chapter 15, appeared in the *Revue des Deux-Mondes* on January 1, 1843. The Andalusia through which Gautier traveled after leaving Seville offers superb examples of Moorish architecture, but he makes little mention of them. The Rock of Gibraltar is the last monolith to claim his attention, and his evocation of it completes the symbolic itinerary of the *récit de voyage.*

> ... c'est un monolithe monstrueux lancé du ciel, un morceau de planète écornée tombé là pendant une bataille d'astres, un fragment du monde cassé ... l'on dirait un sphinx de granit énorme, démesuré, gigantesque, comme pourraient en tailler les Titans qui seraient sculpteurs, et auprès duquel les monstres camards de Karnak et de Giseh sont dans la proportion d'une souris à un éléphant. L'allongement des pattes forme ce qu'on appelle la pointe d'Europe; la tête, un peu tronquée, est tournée vers l'Afrique, qu'elle semble regarder avec une attention rêveuse et profonde. Quelle pensée peut avoir cette montagne à l'attitude sournoisement méditative? Quelle énigme propose-t-elle ou cherche-t-elle à deviner? Les épaules, les reins et la croupe s'étendent vers l'Espagne à grands plis nonchalants, en belles lignes onduleuses comme celle des lions au repos. (*VE* 361)

This evocation recalls earlier ones in which the subject invites comparison with grotesquely immense and exotic forms of life. Here again Gautier indulges his penchant for the theatrical. The difference between Gautier's vision of the Seville cathedral and that of the Rock of Gibraltar is one of degree rather than of kind. In the latter, the stage is simply larger and the principals more bizarre. The narrator's questions make of him a spectator waiting for the curtain to rise, for the last act to begin. These final passages, doubtless written in December of 1842, describe a journey completed in September of 1840, at which point Gautier had composed only six of the forty poems of *España* and had described his unsettling tour of the Escorial for *La Presse*.[1] Gautier's account of his departure towards the end of 1842 betrays an energy and impatience absent from most of the *feuilletons* of 1840. In *Voyage en Espagne* stone is no longer the analogue of a repressive ideal; it bends to the exigencies of a more popular art form. What had been resolved for the narrator of *Voyage en Espagne,* however—the confidence to recreate according to his own vision, and particularly his comic vision—was not immediately apparent in the case of the poet opposed to *le rire*.[2] In *España* the thematics of stone would evolve into a thematics of *difficulté vaincue* that would accommodate *le sourire,* but the process would be revealed gradually in the years to come.

By 1843 Gautier had abandoned the mountaintop. Its context and scale diminished, his poetry would become less populated. There would be few kings, poets, or wanderers to brood alone in monasteries, deserts, and on hilltops. Feeling would be increasingly externalized, confined to objects and events, the poet often absent from his poem.[3] The seven poems of 1843 are for the most part somber, and some are even backward-looking in their use of gothic conventions and older themes. Most of them are in a sense borrowed, either *transpositions d'art* or adaptations of Spanish verse forms. "Le Cid et le Juif" is the rhyming of a legend, a condensed adaptation of a romance by Sepulveda.[4] "Séguidille" imitates a Spanish *seguidilla*, a short *poème à forme fixe* usually set to music. At the same time they are all smaller poems, reduced in scope and marked by greater attention to form.

"Stances" and "Les Affres de la mort" are the darkest poems of this year. They recall Gautier's early gothic efforts but are formally more complex. The extended forms that served his gloomier narratives have been shortened and composed in quatrains. "Stances" is not particulary Spanish in inspiration, and it relies upon commonplace romantic figures. "Les Affres de la mort," however, which iterates the admonition on a cloister wall that denies life and life after death, is not without levity. Though Gautier had little use for the macabre detail peculiar to Spanish realism, he uses it here almost playfully. The stone slab that traumatized him in Goya's "Y aun no se van" is minimized here: "…cette dalle / Qu'aujourd'hui . . . tu soufflettes de ta sandale, / Demain pèsera sur ton corps!" (*PC* 2, 317). More important, the poem's octosyllabic lines and uneven rhythms do not accommodate its grandiloquence, and the mismatch has ironic implications. The poet's sprightly handling—dancing rhythms, teasing alliterations, the absence of rhetoric—of the horrifying prospects he details leavens the gravity of his message. His detachment (he casts himself as the reader) also suggests that he warns with tongue in cheek. Like *Albertus,* this poem is playful, but less ponderously so.[5]

The tone of "Sur le Prométhée du Musée de Madrid," published a few months later, is unequivocal. Bitterness permeates this transposition, a canvas by the seventeenth-century painter Ribeira, as it does Gautier's other critiques of Spanish realism: "Deux tableaux de Valdès Léal," "A Zurbaran," and "Ribeira." These denunciations of an art that Gautier refused to call art occupy a curious place in *España.* Gautier condemned realism in Spanish painting,[6] and these four poems are essentially poetic diatribes. In the context of Gautier's more immediate concerns, they are digressions, though they are examples of the poet's preference for traditional poetic forms. "Sur le Prométhée du Musée de Madrid," however, is more than a *transposition d'art.* It is a recapitulation of the ground covered. There is the same figured opposition of the enduring to the ephemeral; there is also Prometheus, the poet-hero of earlier poems, and there is his mountain. But he is no longer the weakling of "Le Poète et la foule" or the sulk of "Le Roi solitaire." The downward retreat in poems like "Le Poète et la foule," and "Dans la Sierra" is paralleled by a similar progression here: there is a falling into darkness, a movement away from the heights earlier associated with divinity, and there is the same call of distress that is central to "In Deserto," yet here Prometheus is exalted[7]:

> Hélas! il est cloué sur les croix du Caucase.
> Le Titan qui, pour nous, dévalisa les cieux!
> Du haut de son calvaire il insulte les dieux.
> Raillant l'Olympien dont la foudre l'écrase.

> Mais du moins, vers le soir, s'accoudant à la base
> Du rocher où se tord le grand audacieux,
> Les nymphes de la mer, des larmes dans les yeux,
> Echangent avec lui quelque plaintive phrase.
>
> Toi, cruel Ribeira, plus dur que Jupiter,
> Tu fais de ses flancs creux, par d'affreuses entailles,
> Couler à flots de sang des cascades d'entrailles!
>
> Et tu chasses le chœur des filles de la mer;
> Et tu laisses hurler, seul dans l'ombre profonde,
> Le sublime voleur de la flamme féconde! (*PC* 2, 272)

The sonnet is a perfect vehicle for its subject, which is both epic and lyric. The broader quatrains recount the ancient saga on a large scale, balancing Prometheus' suffering with consolation, turbulence with calm, the even cadences of the second quatrain with the irregular rhythms of the first. The tercets, five lines of which depict Ribeira as Prometheus' second adversary, threaten this equilibrium.[8] The quatrains confirm Prometheus' grandeur, the tercets Ribeira's meanness. He is contemptuously addressed, shown bent over his victim with his weapon, a chisel—implied by "entailles" (Gautier had originally written "pinceau de fer")—and by the *harmonie imitative* of "plus dur que Jupiter / Tu fais de ces flancs creux . . ." At issue is the mission of the artist, and what Ribeira mutilates the poet exalts in the absence of comforting nymphs. Though essentially didactic, the sonnet indicates, as do the verse adaptations, Gautier's increasing interest in the smaller poetic forms.[9]

"A Madrid," like "Sur le Prométhée du Musée de Madrid," is also a *transposition d'art* and a denunciation of realism in art.[10] It is also Gautier's first attempt at a more complex tonality, and it anticipates the poetry of a later age in other respects, notably the poetry of Baudelaire.[11] The poem consists of two twelve-line stanzas, the first expository, the second dramatic, and it describes the necrophilic flirtation of a young marquise with a sculpted head:

> Dans le boudoir ambré d'une jeune marquise,
> Grande d'Espagne, belle, et d'une grâce exquise,
> Au milieu de la table, à la place des fleurs,
> Frais groupe mariant et parfums et couleurs,
> Grimaçant sur un plat une tête coupée,
> Sculptée en bois et peinte, et dans le sang trempée,
> Le front humide encor des suprêmes sueurs,
> L'œil vitreux et blanchi de ces pâles lueurs
> Dont la lampe de l'âme en s'éteignant scintille,
> D'une vérité telle et d'un si fin travail,
> Qu'un bourreau n'aurait su reprendre un seul détail.
>
> La marquise disait:—Voyez donc quel artiste!
> Nul sculpteur n'a jamais fait les saint Jean-Baptiste
> Et rendu les effets du damas sur un col
> Comme ce Sévillan, Michel-Ange espagnol!
> Quelle imitation dans ces veines tranchées,
>
> Où le sang perle encore en gouttes mal séchées!
> Et comme dans la bouche on sent le dernier cri
> Sous le fer jaillissant de ce gosier tari!—
> En me disant cela d'une voix claire et douce,
> Sur l'atroce sculpture elle passait son pouce,
> Coquette, souriant d'un sourire charmant,
> L'œil humide et lustré comme pour un amant. (*PC* 2, 270)

The polarities that are constants in Gautier's earlier poetry have changed. The oppositions in this poem are no longer between the mutable and the immutable, but between the pious and the erotic: Gautier has placed the saint's head in a boudoir rather than in a church. Like Baudelaire, Gautier seeks to unsettle and tease his reader by flirting with the scabrous, exposing lust where piety is affected. The opposition is more pointed in the second stanza, which charts the stages of two passions, the one noble, the other ignoble: the marquise is moved by the worldly rather than the otherworldly, by the flesh of the man rather than by the spirit of the saint.

Gautier's conviction that realism in art is not a means of transforming the world but of sinking deeper into it is implied in the leaden rhetoric of martyrdom. "Suprêmes sueurs," "pâles lueurs," "lampe de l'âme" oppress where the sprightly—"frais groupe mariant et parfums et couleurs"—delights. The knife that draws forth "le dernier cri . . . jaillissant" from a "gosier tari" is no less barbaric than Montañès' tool, and it recalls Ribeira's destructive "pinceau de fer." Gautier's use of rhythm to reinforce the tensions between refinement and vulgarity suggests that he now strove for more complex rhythmic and tonal effects. The marquise's proud carriage is replicated in the stately cadences of "Grande d'Espagne, belle, et d'une grâce exquise," whereas her coarseness prompts the cacophonous "Voyez donc quel artiste! / Nul sculpteur n'a jamais fait les saint Jean-Baptiste." "A Madrid" demonstrates the skill in modulating tone that would distinguish Gautier's later poems. The poet criticizes realism in Spanish art more obliquely here than in other poems, but his bitter and heavy-handed ironies still overshadow the poem's playfulness. Here, as in the case of "Sur le Prométhée du Musée de Madrid," one has the impression that Gautier is more critic than poet, and that he had yet to find a subject to celebrate. He would find it before the year was out in the gardens of the Alhambra.

"Le Laurier du Généralife" is one of the few happy poems of *España*. The old tensions between static and dynamic, eternal and ephemeral, are balanced in this tribute to a flowering shrub as a rose laurel is transformed by the ambient water and light. The poem is a variation on the myth of Pygmalion, the illusion being that of a statue come to life.[12] In embracing it, the poet embraces his own creation.

> Dans le Généralife, il est un laurier-rose,
> Gai comme la victoire, heureux comme l'amour.
> Un jet d'eau, son voisin, l'enrichit et l'arrose;
> Une perle reluit dans chaque fleur éclose,
> Et le frais émail vert se rit des feux du jour.
>
> Il rougit dans l'azur comme une jeune fille;
> Ses fleurs, qui semblent vivre, ont des teintes de chair.
> On dirait, à le voir sous l'onde qui scintille,
> Une odalisque nue attendant qu'on l'habille,
> Cheveux en pleurs, au bord du bassin au flot clair.
>
> Ce laurier, je l'aimais d'une amour sans pareille;
> Chaque soir, près de lui, j'allais me reposer;
> A l'une de ses fleurs, bouche humide et vermeille,
> Je suspendais ma lèvre, et parfois, ô merveille!
> J'ai cru sentir la fleur me rendre mon baiser . . . (*PC* 2, 296)

In "Le Laurier du Généralife" the old antitheses recur but in a new and positive guise. In this poem water both crystallizes and animates as the rose-laurel becomes jewel and "jeune fille." Here the artist's changing vision is the measure of his art. As the illusion becomes more complete, the piece more finished, the poet abandons simile for metaphor and the shrub becomes an odalisque. The poem is a tiny drama reminiscent of the myth of Pygmalion. The quality of the poet's emotion changes as his approach—and his poetry—turn the laurel's mirth into reserve and eventually, requited love. Though markedly less studied than the poems of that collection, "Le Laurier du Généralife" looks ahead to *Emaux et Camées*. It is no longer concerned with man or even with the poet, except insofar as it is mildly narcissistic. The poems of 1844 would also attest to Gautier's increased attention to form. With few exceptions, they would no longer contemplate universal issues. As they came closer to exemplifying the "absolute" work of art (*la poésie pure*), their subjects would focus increasingly upon *le non-moi*.

Chapter VIII
The Last Year

MOST OF THE NINE POEMS WRITTEN in 1844 were inspired by Spanish landscapes, paintings, or songs, and they impress chiefly by their diversity of form.[1] By this time Gautier had abandoned even his modified version of the romantic narrative poem and would devote his energies almost exclusively to adaptations. With perhaps one or two exceptions, these poems conform to poetic models for which there is a prescribed stanzaic or metrical pattern. Though Gautier would write little poetry in the five years after he finished *España*—he would in fact bid a formal adieu to his muse—most of the poems of 1844 are prototypical of his later poetry. "A Zurbaran" and "Ribeira," like "Deux Tableaux de Valdès Léal," are extended diatribes in terza rima against the Spanish religious sensibility as he perceived it in certain paintings. Gautier found Zurbaran's brush as unforgiving as Ribeira's, though in his poem entitled "Ribeira," he concedes a certain "volupté" to the painter's expression of suffering.[2] "Le Soupir du More," a shortened adaptation of a Spanish *romance*, recalls the happier visions of *España*, the Andalusian paradises evoked in "Sérénade," "Les Trois Grâces de Grenade," and "Le Laurier du Généralife." "Perspective," another variation on the romantic theme of misunderstood genius, was inspired by the architecture of Seville. "Pendant la tempête" rhymes the simple prayer of sailors threatened by shipwreck.[3] This poem, as well as "Ribeira" and "A Zurbaran," are examples of his increased attention to accent and rhythm.

The two poems of this year that best demonstrate Gautier's increased attention to the "*épithète sonore*" are also adaptations of the Spanish *copla,* a Spanish ballad or drinking song. What distinguishes them from other borrowings is their playful tone, itself largely a function of rhythm. The *mélange des contraires* that Gautier came to defend in prose and in dramatic art admitted all extremes and all intensities of the comic and the sublime. Such was not quite the case with his poetry, even in a parody like *Albertus,* in which opulence as a satirical weapon is blunted by its very lushness. As noted earlier, Gautier was opposed to *le rire* but not to *le sourire* in poetry. In *España,* both "J'allais partir . . ." ("Le fil d'or") and "La Lune" perpetuate the experiment with tonal variety begun in "A Madrid," but there is a difference: where in "A Madrid" Gautier has something serious to say, "J'allais partir" and "La Lune" are frivolous. These poems dance, they play, they tease, they flirt, they mystify.[4]

Both are also examples of the miniaturist at work. They are *microcosmes,* reduced in scope and in scale. In this respect and in their tonal subtlety, the two poems are direct antecedents of *Emaux et Camées*. Their lines are short and their syntax compressed. The first composed, "J'allais partir"—later named "Le Fil d'or"—takes its subject from a romance and its form from the *copla de pie quebrado,*[5] whose stanza is built upon three rhymes, and consists of two couplets of eight syllables alternating with two lines of four syllables. The poem describes a lady's efforts to detain her lover:

> J'allais partir; doña Balbine
> Se lève et prend à sa bobine
>   Un long fil d'or;
> A mon bouton elle le noue,
> Et puis me dit, baisant ma joue:
>   —Restez encor!

> Par l'un des bouts ce fil, trop frêle
> Pour retenir un infidèle,
>   Tient à mon cœur...
> Si vous partez, mon cœur s'arrache;
> Un nœud si fort à vous m'attache,
>   O mon vainqueur!
>
> —Pourquoi donc prendre à ta bobine
> Pour me fixer, doña Balbine,
>   Un fil doré?
> A ton lit qu'un cheveu m'enchaîne,
> Se brisât-il, sois-en certaine,
>   Je resterai! (*PC* 2, 300)

    This poem, which gently satirizes courtly conventions, captures a bit of play in a seamstress's bedroom, and its charm owes much to modulations in tone. It plays upon the cliché "prisoner of love," whose chains are here reduced to the seamstress's thread. The "bout" (du fil) in line seven serves as a transition between the sprightly first stanza and the mock-heroic second stanza, which burlesques hyperbole. In the third stanza, the spirit of the first stanza is temporarily restored, as the lover opposes his playful "*tu*" to doña Balbine's grandiloquent "*vous.*" At the end, the restraint is "*un cheveu,*" rather than, say, "*chevelure.*" The poet-lover gently mocks doña Balbine's exaggerated rhetoric with "*m'enchaîne,*" recalling the original cliché. His rapid (and ungrammatical) shift from imperfect subjunctive to future indicative confirms his appetite if not his devotion.

    Rhythm and sound support these shifts in tone. The brief lines contain as many as four syntactic units whose accents, crowded together, replicate the rapid staccato movements of needle and bobbin. These make for an erotic basso continuo, much strengthened by alliteration, that travesties the nobler sentiments of the piece.[6] The close progression of stops in the first stanza effects a *bégayage* that also adds to the comedy. These plosives give way to fricatives (lines

7-9) that help the expression of delicacy. These in turn yield to a succession of resonant liquids that intensify the mock lyricism of lines 10-12. Such shifts in sound are appropriate to doña Balbine's changing tactics: she is by turns bold, fearful, and passionate—the ellipsis in line nine prepares us for the subsequent shift to melodrama—in her efforts to detain a lover who needs no urging to stay. The first three lines of the third stanza musically replicate the first half of the first stanza, whereas the last three lines but one mimic doña Balbine's lyric plaint at the end of the second stanza.

The appeal of "J'allais partir . . . ," then, derives as much from its sonorities and rhythms as from its visual effects. Where the *microcosmes* of Gautier's earlier poetry impress most by their concentration of the pictorial—"*l'épithète qui peint*"—the later poems of *España* rely increasingly upon "*l'épithète sonore.*" There is in fact in this poem very little by way of visual imagery and certainly no hint of *le thème minéral*. It celebrates the episodic and ephemeral, and its fragile and ironic preciosity are primarily a function of sound. Yet it is an example of sculpting "ce bloc de la phrase," of difficulty overcome.

Where "J'allais partir . . ." borrows from the repertory of a singing muletier, the provenance of "La Lune" is both popular and literary, owing some of its rhymes to Hugo's "A un passant."[7] It also appeals more to the visual imagination than does the earlier poem. "La Lune" is possibly the least spontaneous of *España*, in that the extant manuscripts reveal at least seven reworkings of a stanza. It has the aura of a discreetly whispered exchange in the corner of an eighteenth-century salon, and its charm owes much to the incongruity of its aristocratic principals, sun and moon. Like "J'allais partir . . ." it is playful, and more whimsical than satirical:

>Le soleil dit à la lune:
>—Que fais-tu sur l'horizon?
>Il est bien tard, à la brune,
>Pour sortir de sa maison.

L'honnête femme, à cette heure,
Défile son chapelet,
Couche son enfant qui pleure,
Et met la barre au volet.

Le follet court sur la dune;
Gitanas, chauves-souris,
Rôdent en cherchant fortune;
Noirs ou blancs, tous chats sont gris.

Des planètes équivoques
Et des astres libertins,
Croyant que tu les provoques,
Suivront tes pas clandestins.

La nuit, dehors on s'enrhume.
Vas-tu prendre encor ce soir
Le brouillard pour lit de plume
Et l'eau du lac pour miroir?

Réponds-moi. —J'ai cent retraites
Sur la terre et dans les cieux,
Monsieur mon frère; et vous êtes
Un astre bien curieux! (*PC* 2, 297)

The poem describes a contest between the forces of light and half-light in the form of a squabble between two siblings. As in "J'allais partir . . . ," the general effect of the poem, which here is impressionistic, is a function of shifts in tone. The sun's arguments suggest a tenuous authority, which in turn suggests fluctuations in the quality and intensity of light. In the first and second stanzas he imposes, his strictures delivered in measured cadences. In stanza three, an extended *chuchotement,* he grows dim as the demi-monde of night comes to life. He shines forth again in the fourth stanza, where his latinate diction adds weight to his censure, but in the fifth stanza he recedes with a whine, and at the end disappears as the moon "rises" with her own rebuke. In "La Lune," then, conversational tone translates into quality of light. These synaesthetic correspondances would become fundamental to Symbolist poetry.[8]

Gautier's use here of the *vers impair* unsettles further the already unsettling mood and ambiance created by the poem's shadowy images.[9] It is this unorthodoxy, as well as what has been called the musicality of much of his poetry, that has led several commentators to remark on his affinity to the Symbolists. Serge Fauchereau notes, "On veut tellement voir le peintre en Gautier qu'on oublie de remarquer la musicalité des vers. Cette caractéristique n'avait pas échappé à Hector Berlioz . . ." (Fauchereau 68).[10] Rhythmically "La Lune" is not quite the art of Verlaine: it is too pulsating, too accentual. Though its "music" is more impressionistic than baroque—its alliterations in particular serving the indistinct rather than the distinct—the poet of "La Lune" is not the poet of "Clair de lune." Gautier's visions of cosmic Don Juans and nocturnal predators are theatrical: they spring from a comic as well as from a lyric impulse. His mingling of sense impressions, at least in the poetry of *España*, does not tend towards melancholy as does Verlaine's. (Verlaine's debt to Gautier is, however, considerable, as Fauchereau observes: "On oublie trop ce que les *Fêtes galantes* doivent à *Emaux et Camées*" [115].) But in its celebration of the indeterminate, in particular the chiaroscuro of nocturnal settings and presences, "La Lune" is manifestly unparnassian.

Gautier's preoccupation with the old antitheses is absent from "La Lune" and "J'allais partir. . . ." In addition there is in both poems less emphasis upon color and texture and more upon the effects of rhythm and sound. These efforts lack the rich plastic quality and the satirical verve of *Albertus*, but they exploit the same *mélange des contraires*. Both are essentially theatrical: "J'allais partir . . ." is more akin to a *vaudeville* whereas "La Lune," a slightly more elevated bit of comic badinage, brings to mind the theater of Musset.[11] The gaity of "La Lune" and "J'allais partir . . ." would find its way into Gautier's later poetry, but that gaity would be more subdued. In most instances it would take the form of extremely delicate and muted ironies, for example, in "Variations sur le carnaval de Venise," "Coquetterie posthume," "La Montre," and "La Bonne soirée" (*Emaux et Camées*), and in "Sonnet-dédicace" and "La Vraie esthétique" (*Un Douzain de sonnets*).

With the exception of "A Zurbaran" and "Ribeira," the poems of 1844 are happy ones. They certainly do not prepare us for the bitterness of *España*'s last four poems, especially of "En passant près d'un cimetière" and "Adieux à la poésie." The first of these reduces life to a part played out in a rented costume:

> Qu'est-ce qu'un tombeau?—Le vestiaire où l'âme,
> Au sortir du théâtre et son rôle joué,
> Dépose ses habits d'enfant, d'homme ou de femme,
> Comme un masque qui rend un costume loué! (*PC* 2, 285)

Gautier's nihilism resurfaces in these lines. The dentals in line three replicate the sound of dropped shoes and hammered nails. The actor has finished for the day and for life, and there is the added implication that art is fraudulent—"loué." "Adieux à la poésie," however, would have been more aptly entitled "Au revoir à la poésie," since Gautier would, fortunately, continue to write poetry:

> Allons, ange déchu, ferme ton aile rose;
> Ote ta robe blanche et tes beaux rayons d'or;
> Il faut, du haut des cieux où tendait ton essor,
> Filer comme une étoile, et tomber dans la prose.
>
> Il faut que sur le sol ton pied d'oiseau se pose.
> Marche au lieu de voler: il n'est pas temps encor;
> Renferme dans ton cœur l'harmonieux trésor;
> Que ta harpe un moment se détende et repose.

> O pauvre enfant du ciel, tu chanterais en vain
> Ils ne comprendraient pas ton langage divin;
> A tes plus doux accords leur oreille est fermée!
>
> Mais, avant de partir, bon bel ange à l'œil bleu,
> Va trouver de ma part ma pâle bien-aimée,
> Et pose sur son front un long baiser d'adieu! (*PC* 2, 320)

The poem implicates poet and reader, recalling the difficulties expressed in earlier poems, especially in "Le Roi solitaire," and in "In Deserto." But Gautier's *ange* plays an uncertain part in this poem; must she descend because the poet cannot write, or because he refuses to write? She is told to remove her old equipment, the pink, white, and gold of earlier visions, but to keep her musical instrument for later use. She is further instructed to bid *adieu* not to all poetry but to the languishing romantic model ("ma pâle bien-aimée"). This sonnet, then, is a farewell only to a certain kind of poetry and it stands—by virtue of its form if for no other reason—as a reconfirmation of Gautier's essential classicism.[12] The inspiration for this poem was doubtless also in part Gautier's fatigue, as Jasinski suggests; the *poétique* tentatively proposed in *España* needed time to take root.[13] The retreat anticipated long ago in "La Thébaïde" was not limited to his brief exile in Spain or to the years during which he composed *España;* it included the longer period of withdrawal foretold in "Adieux à la poésie."

Finally, two other poems included in *España* postdate "Adieux à la poésie." "Letrilla" and "J'ai laissé sur mon sein de neige" describe a pain not fully diagnosed. Composed in 1845,[14] both are adaptations of Spanish *coplas,* despite the title of the first, "Letrilla," which designates a longer and sprightlier poem than the *copla*.[15] "J'ai laissé sur mon sein de neige" conveys the simple lyric charm of the Spanish original, but "Letrilla" is the adaptation of two separate and unrelated *coplas*, which the poet may have jotted down together and later consulted as a single composition. Jasinski's criticisms of it are revealing: "Les retouches successives montrent comment il a cherché, avec plus ou moins de bonheur, une unité un peu factice. Un moment, il s'est mal défendu d'un sentimentalisme trop romantique. La seconde strophe, où il devait le plus ajouter, est celle où il a tâtonné le plus" (Jasinski, *L'España* 201). He also mistranslated a word that confuses the "parure" of the first stanza: "il a laissé au mot clave son sens ordinaire de clef, [as opposed to "ardillon"] d'où le détail étrange 'ta clef d'argent à ta ceinture' " (200). All of this, particularly the oversight in translation and some unfinished reworkings of other Spanish poems assumed to have been written in the summer of 1845,[16] suggests that Gautier had neither his mind nor his heart in his work.

Three years would elapse before Gautier set to work on *Emaux et Camées*.[17] The year 1842 confirmed his farewell to romanticism, at least to the expansive romantic genre that Hugo had perfected. With his complex mingling of visual and tonal effects in the poems of 1843-44, he had broken new ground: he had succeeded in producing vaudeville in verse form, but his voice was still tentative. Jasinski observes, "Durant trois années, tout en répandant sa prose opulente, il gardera secret 'l'harmonieux trésor.' Mais ce long silence sera décisif, et sa harpe 'reposée' ne sonnera plus comme avant. Les notes en seront plus pures, plus cristallines, plus grêles un peu dans leur transparence. Son âme y chantera, mais à mi-voix, et comme en écho" (Jasinski, *L'España* 271).[18] Jasinski, then, concedes that despite the "enthousiasme et presque un 'romantisme rajeunis'" of *España,* something had been lost (*PC* 1, lxxi). When Gautier decided definitively to lower his sights, exchanging the heady altitudes of the mountaintop for the calm of the garden and salon, he would write with more confidence but in an increasingly narrowed field of vision. He would turn away from the larger world, sidestepping its roughness and intractability. In doing so, he would point the way for a new poetics.

Chapter IX

España Revisited

RECENT COMMENTATORS HAVE DONE much to correct the notion that Gautier's poetry is without feeling.[1] The lyricism of his ostensibly impassive art has been convincingly demonstrated, and at times virtually quantified, but the poems of *España*—consequently the poetic dialogue that confirmed the complex lyricism of Gautier's mature poetics—have been largely ignored. Gautier's poetry of the late thirties and especially "Départ" reveal a poet in search of renewal and the resolution of half-formulated doubts. The poems of *España* written before 1843, particularly "In Deserto," are evidence of his dilemma. That dilemma, which had persisted as long as Gautier's muse was also his demon, was resolved when the source of the poem's lyricism became its form—"ce bloc de la phrase." Mineral structures and substances were no longer perceived as analogues of immortality. Relatedly, the notion of a poetic absolute dictating what David Burnett has called Gautier's "édifices poétiques" no longer obtained.[2] Between 1840 and 1845 Gautier evolved from architect, whose raw materials often served the expression of diffuse and platitudinous sentiments, to *bijoutier,* crafter of textures and sonorities. The cloisters, towers, and graveyards of the earlier poems of *España* were reduced to the simple tomb of "En passant près d'un cimetière"; the panoramic vistas of northern Spain condensed into the Andalusian vision of "Le Soupir du More" and the dense stone cluster of "Perspective." The broad forms congenial to romantic parody and lament had yielded gradually to smaller ones whose prosodic devices were better suited to the discreet ironies and nostalgias of *Emaux et Camées*. The lyricism of his octosyllabic poems in 1843 and 1844—especially "J'allais partir . . ." and "La lune"— is musical and cinematic; it inheres in the world of *le non-moi*.[3] The emotion inspired by these and later poems would be primarily esthetic.[4]

The transitional character of *España* is accordingly not simply a matter of alexandrines reduced to octosyllables or romantic turbulence stilled by Parnassian calm, as some have maintained.[5] It is to be found in the self-conscious poems that are not yet octosyllabic, but that strive for compression and concentration of effect at the same time that they propose an essentially romantic *matière*. They are the poems in which Gautier tempers the effusions of his romantic peers, whose chorus he has left, with the lapidary's rigor. In these he records for the last time doubts that are private and unshared, and these are always whispered. The immediate appeal in all of these efforts proceeds from the poet's apparent feelings: melancholy, awe, horror, exultation and the like. The veiled tensions of his dilemma, imbedded in the rock and stone of the poem's landscapes and monuments, qualify the superficial emotion, giving it a more complex resonance and complicating the poetic experience. In "Le Poète et la foule" and "J'étais monté plus haut," Gautier confronts mountains that simultaneously beckon and intimidate. In "La Fontaine du cimetière" and "Dans la Sierra" the mineral world helps to dramatize the poet's infirmities and inadequacies. "Le Roi solitaire" adds to these infirmities paralysis and alienation. By 1842 these issues have reached a critical point: they inhere in the minerals, the flora and the fauna of a silent landscape and they provoke the poetic wail of "In Deserto."

But Gautier was slow to abandon the discursive model that served the heart and conscience of his generation, and he did so slowly and *à contre-cœur*. Though demanding of himself, he was never contemptuous of his public.[6] Gautier's principles were rigorous—and there is admittedly much in his poetry that elevates artifice to a point beyond the grasp of the average reader—but they were not necessarily undemocratic. He never regarded art as the sole province of a literary minority: "Est-ce à dire . . . que l'art doive se renfermer dans un indifférentisme de parti-pris, dans un détachement glacial de toute chose vivace et contemporaine pour n'admirer, Narcisse idéal, que sa propre réflexion dans l'eau et devenir amoureux? Non . . . !" (Töppfer 900-901). He embraced humble minds and sensibilities, both rustics and bourgeois, in his own culture as well as in others, and he respected, especially in the former, an instinctive and intuitive esthetic sense (he was particularly admiring of acrobats).[7] He came as close as any poet to regarding language as artifact, and while the title of his best-known work, *Emaux et Camées,* implies rare substances, he respected the humblest artisan, and his standard of judgment was derived from relatively primitive art forms: "Il y a trois choses qui sont pour moi des thermomètres précis de l'état de civilisation d'un peuple: la poterie, l'art de tresser soit l'osier soit la paille, et la manière de harnacher les bêtes de somme" (*VE* 105). These criteria are evidence of the broad taste and democratic sympathies that complicated his attitudes, particularly in the early 1840s. He hardly regarded art as an instrument of social reform, nor should it be forgotten that poetry was not Gautier's livelihood. He earned his living addressing a public from which he and his peers often felt alienated. This was by and large the bourgeois readership of *La Presse* and similar publications who generally expected deep feelings and high morals of their writers and were often as deaf to the subtleties of poetry as they were alert to its occasional indecencies.

He sought to reach, and did reach, a public unbound by the scruples of respectability, one who welcomed the exuberance and Gallic wit of the author of *Albertus, Mademoiselle de Maupin,* and *Les Grotesques,* to name a few of the works, most of them prose, that are neither discreet nor, in the case of *Albertus,* exemplary of his eventual poetics.[8] The narrator of *Voyage en Espagne* is that of the genial and occasionally irreverent host, the traveler who addresses his reader as though he were a guest, taking him by the arm to guide him from the cathedral to the nearest *venta* for a meal and livelier entertainment. Here was a man who enjoyed the pleasures and company of the least of men, for these experiences were as valuable as any to the writer. Herein lies perhaps the supreme irony of Gautier's plight: his outgoing nature and his liberal temperament must have played some part in developing the lexical brilliance of his mature poetry. Georges Matoré writes: "si on peut reprocher à certains néologismes de Gautier de n'être pas indispensables, on ne peut que louer l'auteur de *Mademoiselle de Maupin* de n'avoir créé ou utilisé que des mots 'conformes au génie de la langue et imprégnés de la saveur du terroir gaulois' " (Matoré, *Vocabulaire* 191). But Gautier's appreciation of the *génie de la langue gauloise* did not, unfortunately, guarantee his poetry the wider public success he hoped for.

Perhaps the the most telling evidence of Gautier's attitudes—at least in the 1840s—is to be found in a review he wrote of the Théâtre des Funambules shortly after he published "In Deserto." It is Gautier's most explicit defense of an art he greatly admired:

> L'auteur de ces merveilleuses parades c'est tout le monde; . . . c'est le souffleur, le public surtout, qui fait ces sortes de pièces à peu près comme ces chansons pleines de fautes de mesures et de rime qui font le désespoir des grands écrivains, et pour un couplet desquelles ils donneraient, avec de retour, leurs strophes les plus précisément ciselées. (Souvenirs 56)[9]

There can be no doubt that it was he himself he was writing of in these lines. Here was an art to all appearances effortless if not spontaneous, an art less exalted than his own yet one whose heights he had not reached. The paradox is striking. Gautier's failure to speak to all men—to be that desert spring "Où les pâtres conduiraient leurs troupeaux"—is in part the subject of "In Deserto," the last poem in which he entertains the possibility of an epic role. The art of Gautier's mature poetry is a confident art, the art of a poet aware of his strengths, as Gabriel Brunet has maintained, and though readers now accord him the respect given him earlier by poets alone, it is late in coming.[10] But the achievement of his later years did not entirely heal the wounds of the 1830s and 1840s. Paolo Tortonese, for one, has observed: "Lui-même a connu, vers la fin de sa vie, le sentiment aigu d'avoir été mal compris" (Tortonese 80).[11] Léon Cellier's qualified appreciation of the writer—"Gautier 'maître et ombre' est un écrivain d'avenir, non pas tant parce qu'il fut un poète impeccable, que parce que son angoisse sut se masquer sous les dehors de l'humour et du fantastique" (Cellier, "Gautier, un écrivain" 4)—might have been more justly phrased to echo those of Baudelaire and Barbey d'Aurevilly—"Gautier 'maître et ombre' est un poète d'avenir dont l'angoisse sut se masquer sous les dehors de l'humour et du fantastique."

Notes

Introduction

[1] It is generally conceded that *España* marks the end of Gautier's efforts to emulate the older generation of romantics. P. E. Tennant observes, "This [*España*] was to be almost the last time Gautier treated wider philosophical or human problems in direct poetic form, either sustaining argument at length or compressing it sharply into vivid, symbolic form" (Tennant 57). Gautier himself, in a letter to Sainte-Beuve in 1838, wrote that he had renounced subjective inspiration for greater objectivity (Spoelberch de Lovenjoul 1, 105-6), and it is also true that shorter forms and his use of the octosyllable predominate in *España* and in subsequent collections. See Van der Tuin, 266, and chapter 1 of this study.

[2] Laurence Porter, *The Crisis of French Symbolism*, 3. See 9-13 for his discussion of the unreliability of language and the impossibility of transcendence.

[3] "Fuyez toujours l'épithète musicale pour l'épithète qui peint." Théophile Gautier, as reported in Arsène Houssaye's *Les Confessions. Souvenirs d'un demi-siècle littéraire* 5, 86. "Sonore" would be a more appropriate qualifier; see chapter 8, note 10.

Chapitre I : Gautier *poète*

[1] Lanson even hailed *España* as "le vrai commencement du naturalisme" (Lanson 228). Faguet contended that Gautier was "dépourvu d'idées, de sensibilité" (Faguet, *Le XIXe siècle,* 295), while Lanson claimed que he had "renoncé au lyrisme subjectif pour s'asservir à l'objet" (Lanson 967).

[2] See John Houston's remarks on the subject in his *French Symbolism and the Modernist Movement*, 10.

[3] He adds "Allons plus loin: il y a la tendance de l'image à se séparer de l'idée, pour vivre d'elle-même d'une vie propre et indépendante," which is doubtless what Gautier meant it to do. (It should be noted that most of Brunetière's examples are taken from Gautier's early period and that these are not typical

of his later efforts.) Gabriel Brunet, writing almost thirty years later in 1922, concurred with Brunetière, echoing Sainte-Beuve: "Comme il ne fait pas intervenir les forces cachées et profondes, le mouvement qu'il crée reste en surface" (Brunet 318).

[4] These critics judged as representative poems in which the poetic vision is followed by abstract commentary. It is true that in some instances superfluous comment is added to the poem, but this is not often the case. It is only occasionally true of the early poetry, and not at all of *España*. (Of Brunetière's observation that Gautier could not "fondre la matière et l'idée du poème," Van der Tuin comments that it would apply to only a number of Gautier's poems [Van der Tuin 47]). See also G. Brunet 326-27.

[5] Van der Tuin contends that later, in his "strong" period, Gautier adopted the octosyllabic line as an ally against sentimentality: "Jusqu'ici—nous avons dépassé la date de *L'España*—Gautier traduisait ses idées, ses sentiments en général dans des rythmes larges, mouvementés, en harmonie avec les plaintes romantiques, plus ou moins factices, de son cœur. . . . En 1844, Gautier se sent attiré plus fortement vers l'octosyllabe, c'est-à-dire que la prédilection qu'il avait inconsciemment pour ce vers pénètre dans sa conscience claire" (Van der Tuin 266). Van der Tuin assigns no role to *España* in the evolution of Gautier's poetics. The volume would have belonged to Gautier's romantic period, and its emotions would have been for the most part "contrived": "Cette période s'est concrétisée dans la forme servant de point d'appui, de soutien pour lutter contre la négativité. En d'autres termes, Gautier avait trouvé la non-sentimentalité, le repos stoïque dans la forme froide et dure, où pouvait s'exprimer son esthétique 'isolée,' de très faible dynamisme, sans chaleur vitale, détachée de la vie, envers laquelle il prenait une attitude contemplative, 'sans intérêt' " (267).

[6] Poet Yvor Winters is one. In a discussion of Herrick's poems on the subject of the mortality of man and the immortality of art, he writes: "They are in a classical tradition that has continued almost into our own time: the finest poem on the subject within the past century and a half is *L'Art,* by Théophile Gautier. This poem has far greater intellectual content than the poems by Herrick, and is at least as well written. We tend to think of Gautier as a minor poet, and perhaps he was, but perhaps we should reread him. If he was a minor poet, he was a minor poet in one of the greatest periods of occidental literature, the French period from Gautier through Valéry" (Winters 112).

[7] The phrase is G. Brunet's: Gautier's is an "art de surface . . . qui se détourne volontairement des plongées dans la réalité profonde pour se contenter de fixer les apparences du monde" (G. Brunet 303).

[8] Poulet observes, "Excès de richesse plastique, mais excès aussi d'évidence. L'être rêvé semble devenir de plus en plus réel à mesure qu'il devient de plus en plus visible. . . . A force de détailler ses apparences, le poète lui confère non pas sans doute une vérité interne, mais une évidence proprement extérieure, qui se traduit par une qualité que Gautier est presque le seul à posséder parmi les romantiques, et qui est la netteté. Tout se ramène, dans cette progression quantitative et qualitative de l'image, à un passage du flou au net, de l'émotionnel au sensible (et au sensuel), du ressenti au visualisé" (Poulet, *Trois essais* 111). In a later text (*La Pensée Indéterminée* II), Poulet revisits Gautier's insistence upon the durable image, contending that his success lies in the unrealized rather than in the perfected image (119). He adds, "Derrière l'œuvre formée de Gautier, ses poèmes, ses romans, ses pièces de théâtre, il y avait le germe d'une œuvre non formée, osons même le dire, une œuvre proprement informe" (120). But where Poulet persists in denying him originality, Paolo Tortonese, in his tribute to the critic, maintains the contrary: "Au delà de son grand effort de concentration sur l'objet, de son travail de représentation et de concrétisation, Gautier nous fait sentir ce qui échappe encore à la parole humaine. L'image qui se pétrifie, la parole exsangue, ne constituent pas des échecs de Gautier. Ce sont plutôt des mises en scène d'un échec universel, dont il sait nous parler d'une manière unique et surprenante . . ." (Tortonese 79).

[9] Crouzet contends that excess in Gautier's art—the superabundance of tangible "signs" of art—proceeds from a "confiance en un modèle de type formel, en une croissance systématique qui reduit l'invention à une logique et exclut la vérité intérieure et son imprévu" (Crouzet 662). It should be noted, however, that Crouzet focuses primarily upon Gautier's prose.

[10] G. Brunet had also discerned in Gautier a tendency to perceive nature in terms of the works of art he knew well (he called it Gautier's "artisme" [309]), and Rita Benesch observed that "Le regard de Gautier aime à se poser sur les silhouettes de formes et de couleurs variées que présentent les œuvres d'art" (G. Brunet 55).

[11] Crouzet also intuits a fear of inadequacy in Gautier, which he believes influenced his prose in particular. He contends that with Gautier, "le trop plein se rapproche du vide," and he suggests that this "surcharge de l'esthétique" is

compensatory, "comme si l'artiste redoutait une insuffisance" (Crouzet 664). Faguet had noted a similar tendency in Gautier's early poetry: "Et notez qu'elles (les longues méditations) contiennent des demi-pages très remarquables, mais perdues dans un tel vide et dans un vide si péniblement travaillé!" (300).

[12] Article of December 9, 1844, reprinted in *Histoire de l'art dramatique en France depuis vingt-cinq ans* 3, 302. Gautier only once explicitly refers to his work as failed. See Fauchereau 57-58.

[13] See chapter 8. Like Cockerham and Scott, Fauchereau also defends the man of feeling: "Ce serait un contresens de prendre le léger sourire de Gautier comme un signe d'indifférence" (Fauchereau 105). Fauchereau also discusses at some length what he regards as Gautier's ill-deserved reputation in France. He notes that the English have always admired him, and that his influence has extended as far as Russia and Central America, but that in France only students of "la littérature fantastique" have not underestimated his achievement. See 118-22.

[14] Mallarmé had similarly remarked: "La phrase—plastique aux yeux des imbéciles—de Th. Gautier, mais qui, pour moi, est équilibrée miraculeusement, a une justesse de touche qui est de la justice" (Lettre à Henri Cazalis du 15 avril 1864 [Coll. Henri Mondor], 124).

[15] Scott maintains that in most instances the rhythmic ambivalence of the octosyllable denies that periodicity which "consolidates the unicity of the lyric voice and ensures its stamina" (C. Scott 44). The result is a diversified rather than a unified tone. At the same time, however, he finds that in a number of the poems "Gautier seeks to establish a consistency of voice, a lyric momentum which drives through the poem from one end to the other (e.g., 'Diamant du cœur,' 'Premier sourire du printemps,' 'Dernier Vœu')" (44).

[16] *Tableau historique et critique de la poésie française et du théâtre français au XVIe siècle* (1828).

[17] Opposed to such irresponsibility among potentially influential writers were reformers who had been encouraged by the revolution of 1830. The socialistic Ecole saint-simonienne in particular, together with the Fouriéristes, believed that the artist should provide the spiritual impetus necessary for social cohesion and progress. These movements influenced most of the older romantic poets and a few of the younger ones, including some of Gautier's own confrères. The doctrine of art for art's sake was consequently slow to impose itself. After the demise in 1833 of its principal organ, the short-lived

L'Europe littéraire, Hugo retired from the battle, and *L'Artiste,* in spite of its efforts to win public support for artists, hesitated to defend the doctrine too vehemently. It remained for Gautier himself, the most ardent champion of *l'art pour l'art,* to defend its principles. These principles, laid down in the preface to *Mademoiselle de Maupin* (1834) and dramatized in the work itself, would be restated in his well-known poem "l'Art." They would become the new bible of le Parnasse. For a full discussion of the matter, see Jasinski's *Les Années romantiques de Théophile Gautier (Années* 169-217), Matoré's *Préface de 'Mademoiselle de Maupin,'* and Adolphe Boschot's introduction to the Garnier edition of *Mademoiselle de Maupin.*

[18] See Jasinski's edition of Gautier's *Poésies complètes* (*PC,* iii-xvi), for a detailed account of the circumstances of publication of Gautier's early poetry.

[19] See Jasinski's *L' "España" de Théophile Gautier* (*L'España*) 37-38, and his commentaries on the individual poems for a fuller account of the matter. See also Jasinski's edition of the complete poems (*PC*).

[20] See G. Brunet for a discussion of influences in Gautier's "A Mon ami Eugène de N *** (Nully)," a poem from his first published collection; "Victor" and "Sainte-Beuve" are "auteurs chéris." In his *Histoire du romantisme,* Gautier also writes: "dans l'art comme dans la réalité on est toujours fils de quelqu'un" (299). Freeman Henry, in "Relire Théophile Gautier," notes (of Gautier's eclecticism): "Le message esthétique est celui de la régénération perpétuelle des arts et de la littérature grâce à une poétique qui encourage l'hybridation, la mutation savante" (Henry, "Relire," 4).

[21] See Gautier's articles in *La Presse,* 4 April 1839 and in the *Revue de Paris,* April 1841.

[22] See Henri van der Tuin. Gautier's depressions were not always conventionally romantic; Baudelaire may have taken his cue from the following lines:

> Depuis de si longs jours prisonnier, tu t'ennuies,
> Pauvre oiseau, de ne voir qu'intarissables pluies,
> De filets gris rayant un ciel noir et brumeux,
> Que toits aigus baignés de nuages fumeux
> . . . .
> Mon âme est comme toi: de sa cage mortelle
> Elle s'ennuie, hélas! et souffre et bat de l'aile.
>   ("L'Oiseau captif," *PC* 1, 35-6)

"Spleen III," in particular, makes use of almost identical figures to evoke a complex depression: "Où l'Espérance, comme une chauve-souris, / S'en va battant les murs de son aile timide" (*BOC* 1, 74-75).

[23] Joanna Richardson, for example, writes: "Poésies . . . is the work of a writer who . . . still uses all the Gothic impedimenta of stained-glass windows, moonlit basilicas, corpses on gibbets, birds of prey, death's heads and cataracts" (Richardson 22). See also Cockerham 7-13 for a discussion of the innovative aspects of Gautier's early poetry.

[24] Gautier and Baudelaire disagreed on this point. When Baudelaire praised him for "la puissance étonnante qu'il avait montrée dans le bouffon et le grotesque," Gautier replied that "il avait en horreur l'esprit et le rire, ce rire qui déforme la créature de Dieu" (*BOC* 2, 108). Baudelaire later commented: "Quelque léger que cet ouvrage (*Albertus*) puisse paraître à plusieurs, il renferme de grands mérites. Outre la beauté du diable, c'est-à-dire la grâce charmante et l'audace de la jeunesse, il contient le rire, et le meilleur rire. Evidemment, à une époque pleine de duperies, un auteur s'installait en pleine ironie et prouvait qu'il n'était pas dupe" (Fauchereau 48-49). Fauchereau adds: "Il est vrai que la poésie romantique ne nous semble généralement pas compatible avec le rire. Sans être dépourvu d'humour comme Lamartine ou Vigny, Hugo qui peut être fort drôle dans son théâtre est d'un imperturbable sérieux dont il ne se départira que passé la cinquantaine. Il n'y a guère que Musset qui ait su rire" (40). See 41-49 for Fauchereau's complete analysis of Gautier's "diablerie."

[25] Fauchereau observes: "Loin d'être . . . une classique histoire de sorcellerie, c'en est la parodie, exécutée par un virtuose. *Albertus* est le chef-d'œuvre de la littérature frénétique dont il est en même temps une savoureuse démystification. On se place à contresens . . . si l'on aborde *Albertus* comme on aborderait 'le Lac,' l'"Ode à la Colonne' ou 'La Maison du berger,' et si l'on n'a pas envie de rire, il vaut mieux laisser le livre de côté (Fauchereau 39-40) . . . *Albertus* est l'ouvrage où Gautier a le plus laissé cours à sa fantaisie (44) . . . Sans cesse le texte tire la langue au lecteur" (46).

[26] Tennant has noted that in this respect Gautier "presents the same curious dichotomy as Byron or Hoffmann, in whom scepticism and mockery are constant correctives of the lyrical, asserting the dignity of man by affirming his self-control" (Tennant 102). See also Gosselin-Schick 62-63 for a discussion of the poem as "package." David Graham Burnett, in his discussion of the order—and therefore of the role—of "Portail" (in what has traditionally

though uneasily been described as a unity, consisting of "Portail," *La Comédie de la mort,* and "Le Sommet de la tour") has also pointed to the ironist at work as well as to the poet bent upon recognition: "En fin de compte, Gautier ne se fait pas d'illusions sur la capacité de l'artiste de se diviniser. La divinité que confère 'la gloire' sur le poète vient d'autrui. . . . Une conscience ironique de soi comme artiste en train de 'faire' de l'art informe donc la vue retrospective de 'Portail' et du 'Sommet' " (Burnett, "Composition" 6).

[27] Burnett notes of these lines: "Il s'agit donc d'une fonction ironique où la forme est censée tromper l'observateur/lecteur. La fonction de récipient risque de disparaître totalement, car une illusion morte, en fin de compte, n'est plus une illusion du tout. Créer l'illusion de beauté autour d'un espace essentiellement vide pour provoquer la fantaisie esthétique c'est là la tâche avouée du jeune poète" (Burnett, "Metaphore" 46-47). See also Gosselin-Schick 55-56.

[28] The cathedral merits special notice here because of its complex symbolism and precisely because it is inseparable from *la gloire.* David Burnett has described the poet's effort to achieve a privileged view (of the city from the top of the building) as "cette recherche de la gloire au moyen de la cathédrale" (Burnett, "Métaphore" 47). He has observed that Gautier's early poetry struggles with the question of whether the edifice is a "fantasy-generating void" or an "exemplum of the poet's divine mission" (Burnett, "Architecture" 114). Citing "Le Sommet de la tour" (1838) in a later article, he refines upon the notion of the poet-architect, describing Gautier's cathedral as representing both an ideal and a refuge, noting that the poet is both "architecte et locataire de l'édifice poétique" (Burnett, "Métaphore" 46). We will review Burnett's observations later in the context of *España,* in particular his conclusion that the poet's early efforts were "vouée à l'échec" (48) and that in Gautier's later poems there are no more large public buildings such as the cathedral since "l'absence d'un idéal préconçu élimine la nécessité d'une forme fixe dictée par le caractère de cet ideal" (49).

[29] Gosselin-Schick points to the irony in the poet's lengthy expression of his desire to be silent, and to the poem's self-indulgent and romantic textuality. There is in this tendency something of the excess discerned by Crouzet in Gautier's prose, an anxiety generated by the fear of not communicating that results in "overcommunication." One reason Gautier may have abandoned the romantic mode was precisely because he came to distrust its rhetoric.

[30] The words are Tennant's 31.

Chapter II: The Journey to Spain

[1] For a discussion of French travel to Spain, see Bulgin (Koestler), *The Making of an Artist: Gautier's 'Voyage en Espagne,'* 6.

[2] The events of the first quarter of the century had intensified the interest of the French in Spanish affairs, and the press accordingly devoted more space to articles on Spain. The *Journal de Paris* published many of these during the thirties as did *Le Musée des familles,* which also included travelogues. Between 1831 and 1834, *La Revue des Deux Mondes* published a series of travel accounts by Fontaney, Viardot's *Etudes sur l'Espagne,* and soon afterwards Corneille's *Souvenirs d'Espagne,* along with an increasing number of critical pieces on Spanish art, theater, and literature.

[3] Ilse Lipshutz observes, "It was mainly the writers of the avant-garde of the young Romantic movement who first sensed the esthetic enrichment offered by Spanish paintings, where Spain's people, so frequently evoked in their writings, came to life: kings, Virgins, and majas; urchins and decrepit old men" (Lipshutz 149). Lipshutz suggests that Goya's *Caprichos* were largely responsible for the Gothic imagery that informs many works written in the early 1830s, notably Gautier's "Albertus" (118).

[4] "Tous les voyages romantiques sont livresques. Lamartine, Gautier, Nerval, Flaubert, etc., corrigent, complètent, varient le thème posé par Chateaubriand" (Butor 12).

[5] Paul Fussell makes the following distinction between the guide and the travel book: "A guide book is addressed to those who plan to follow the traveler, doing what he has done, but more selectively. A travel book, at its purest, is addressed to those who do not plan to follow the traveler at all, but who require the exotic or comic anomalies, wonders, and scandals of the literary form romance which their own place or time cannot entirely supply. . . . It invites the reader to undertake three tours simultaneously: abroad, into the author's brain, and into one's own" (Fussell 183-84).

[6] Nerval's *Voyage en Orient,* for which Gautier himself wrote a eulogistic preface, is an example of such literary hybridism.

[7] See Cockerham for an account of the circumstances surrounding the publication of Gautier's first volume of poetry (Cockerham 2-3). Fauchereau notes of the cholera epidemic of 1832 that it "avait fait quelque mille victimes—qui ne seront peut-être pas pour rien dans les cadavres de la *Comédie de la mort* et le rire jaune de certains contes des années trente" (Fauchereau 31).

⁸ See A. Fontainas "Les Poésies de Théophile Gautier" (*Mercure de France,* September-October, 1911).

⁹ René Jasinski's study of Gautier's salad days (*Les Années romantiques de Théophile Gautier*) reviews at length the circumstances that would dispose Gautier to flee Paris. Gautier's *Voyage en Espagne* will be discussed in later chapters.

¹⁰ See Bulgin (Koestler), chapter 4.

Chapter III: *España*

¹ The year 1845 also saw the completion of "Deux tableaux de Valdès Léal" which Gautier had expanded and already renamed in 1842. The original, written in 1841, was entitled "Un tableau de Valdès Léal."

² Jasinski concedes as much: "On a pris le recueil tel qu'il s'offre à nous" (Jasinski, *L'España* 35).

³ Michael Levey, in his review "*Théophile Gautier: A Romantic Critic of the Visual Arts*" by Robert Snell, describes them as "an assemblage of dusty, overcultured trinkets" (Levey 434). Gosselin-Schick, taking her lead from Jasinski and others who have shown that *España* does not represent the "real" Spain (Gosselin-Schick 82-84), goes a step further. She contends that "the poems signify something other than Spain" (85) and that *España* is a "means by which Gautier seeks to experience the void of an authorial identity and/or presence, that is, by which he essays death" (87). To say that *España* should be no more than a means of "essaying death" grossly limits and diminishes this poetry, to say the least.

⁴ Claude-Marie Senninger notes "Son esthétique de la prose semble donc en avance . . . sur son esthétique poétique" (Senninger 54).

⁵ Henri van der Tuin has ascribed these perceptions to Gautier's fear of the object. He contends that the poet's excessive introversion led him away from reality, but that "Par une réaction démesurée, d'autant plus forte que l'introversion a été grande, les rôles sont retournés: le moi est mis sous l'empire magique de l'objet. La réalité se venge comme Gautier l'avait craint" (Van der Tuin 145).

⁶ In Gautier's obituary tribute to Jules Goncourt (June 25, 1870) he speaks of a "perpétuelle tension de l'esprit, l'effort sans repos, la lutte avec la difficulté créée à plaisir, la fatigue de rouler ce bloc de la phrase, plus pesant que celui de Sisyphe" (*Portraits Contemporains* 201).

⁷ See Houston 14-26, for a discussion of objectivity as it determines mood.

Chapter IV: The Poems of 1840

[1] The plates Gautier describes are from Goya's *Caprichos*, which he had seen in Paris. Most of his discussion in *Voyage en Espagne* is the verbatim text of an article he had written earlier and published in *La Presse* in 1838 (some of which may have been plagiarized from an article by Baron Taylor [See Michael Spencer's *Art Criticism of Théophile Gautier*, 82-83]). Gautier's inclusion of this material in this section on Madrid is understandable, if only because other work by Goya was displayed in the museum at the time. However, his treatment of the gruesome subjects of the Goya's drawings also argues for the persistence of his *maladie gothique*.

[2] Gautier's account of his unsettling yet exhilarating ride from Madrid to Burgos is a celebration of movement and sound, of an ambulant cacophany, the figurative shout of one no longer intimidated or constrained to silence. See Bulgin (Koestler), 47-48. Francine Court-Perez (*Gautier, un romantique ironique*) notes: "En Espagne, le plaisir du voyage réside en partie dans le déplacement vif" (Court-Perez 217).

[3] Gautier spent much time revising this poem. Jasinski observes that the abbreviated rhythm, compelled by the six-syllable line, "entraînait des difficultés de versification" (Jasinski, *L'España* 101).

[4] François Brunet, in a discussion of Gautier's attitude towards the Escorial ("Posé comme un défi . . .") suggests that he regarded it as "lancé par Philippe II" as a "défi au bon sens, aux lois habituelles de la vie en société et tout particulièrement au mode de vie habituelle dans une monarchie" (F. Brunet 192).

[5] See *L'España* 173 for the original line.

Chapter V: the Poems of 1841

[1] If one reads *Voyage en Espagne* as quest literature, then Gautier's visit to the Escorial is a descent, a figurative burial. In Toledo, he mounts the staircase of the Alcazar, achieving a figurative rebirth. His subsequent dip in the Tagus could then be construed as a figurative baptism.

[2] In these pages Gautier devotes considerable attention to "la garde-robe de la vierge," comparing the Virgin to women less well dressed, placing her in a sort of theatrical competition in which costume will determine the winner. See *VE* 156-57.

[3] "Un Tableau de Valdès Léal" was revised late in 1842 to include a transposition of the companion piece to the first painting (*Finis gloriae mundi*) and retitled

"Deux Tableaux de Valdès Léal" when it was further revised and published in the 1845 edition of *Poésies complètes*. Both canvasses hang in the Residencia de la Santa Caridad in Seville. (See Jasinski, *L'España* 225-31 for further discussion.) Though it does not bear directly on Gautier's poetics, the poem is symptomatic of the poet's state of mind during this period and deserves comment. Like the other morbid poems of 1841, this transposition of *In ictu oculi* opposes the opulence of life to the horror of death. It is the stuff of which *Albertus* is made, except that where wit inspired the one, a bitter animus drives the other. Gautier's evocation of the painting, which depicts a variety of scattered treasures, is at the same time a reproach leveled at the sadistic painter:

> Le premier, toile étrange où manquent les figures,
> N'est qu'un vaste fouillis d'étoffes, de dorures,
> De vases, d'objets d'art, de brocarts opulents,
> Miroités de lumière et de rayons tremblants.
> Tous les trésors du monde et toutes les richesses:
> Les coffres-forts des juifs, les écrins des duchesses,
> Sur de beaux tapis turcs de grandes fleurs brodés,
> Rompant leur ventre d'or, semblent s'être vidés. (*PC* 2, 305-6)

The passage is an extended metaphor for abuse. The poet perceives of the objects in Valdès Léal's still life as vessels, or better wombs, whose contents have been wrenched from them and strewn about. Upon this scene the last to arrive—"le convive importun" (death)—wreaks the ultimate havoc. The rhythms of Gautier's invective are driven by the same anger that inspired "Sur le Prométhée du Musée de Madrid," "A Zurbaran" and "Ribeira."

[4] The subject was hardly original, and Gautier took his lead from a number of earlier poets. Jasinski has uncovered numerous phrases and whole lines from Hugo (*Les Feuilles d'Automne, Les Orientales, Les Rayons et les Ombres*), borrowings from Sainte-Beuve (*Poésies de Joseph Délorme, L'Enfant rêveur*) and from Gautier's *Mademoiselle de Maupin* and earlier poems, all of them expressive of the need for a change of scene (Jasinski, *L'España* 55-60). E. G. Lien includes "Départ" in his article "The Prefatory Poetics of Théophile Gautier," though it was composed later than many of the poems of *España*.

[5] The affinities of "Départ" to Musset's "Nuit de Mai" (1835) are striking, though the arguments differ. It ends on the same abject note, there is a similar dialogue in which the hopeful poet fails to persuade his less hopeful half that

there is reason to persevere, and the form of the poem parallels its effect, though less markedly than with Musset.

[6] Compare "J'effacerais mon nom de ma propre mémoire; . . . Je veux dans le néant renouveler mon être, / M'isoler de moi-même et ne plus me connaître" ("Thébaïde," *PC* 2, 65, 67) with "Je sentais le désir d'être absent de moi-même" (*PC* 1, 252) and "Mais je suis curieux d'essayer de l'absence" (*PC* 1, 254) of "Départ," and also with the passage in *Voyage en Espagne* in which Gautier appears to realize his wish: "il me prenait des doutes sur ma propre identité; je me sentais si absent de moi-même, transporté si loin de ma sphère, que tout cela me paraissait une hallucination, un rêve étrange. . . ." (*VE* 145).

[7] The writing of "Départ" preceded the composition of a group of poems published together in *La Revue des Deux Mondes,* all but two of which have mineral settings. In "En allant à la chartreuse de Miraflorès," a single stanza poem of fourteen lines, the traveler's arduous climb up the rocky approach to the monastery is a simple parallel to the poet's efforts. This poem, by virtue of its lifeless setting, is an apt preface to "La Fontaine du cimetière," which followed it. A later and equally straightforward poem, "Consolation," equates the mountain climber with the aspiring poet as well as with the unwilling reader. But these are minor efforts, abbreviated variations on common romantic elitist themes.

[8] Gautier's revisions to the third stanza have the effect of increasing this tension between movement and inertia. An earlier version contains the following lines:

> Deux *énormes* cyprès à la noire verdure
> *Allongent* tristement leur silhouette dure
> *Dans la sérénité transparente des cieux*
> *Au milieu*—du bassin d'une avare fontaine
> *S'échappe par instant* une nappe incertaine
> Comme des pleurs furtifs qui débordent des yeux.
> (Jasinski, *L'España* 78)

The halting "Au milieu," replaces "énormes," and the static "profilent" replaces "allongent." At the same time, "élancés vers les cieux" conveys movement whereas the prepositional phrases it replaces does not. The choice of "Tombe," rather than "S'échappe" is more appropriate because of its multiple connotations (fall = fail, weaken, die). Finally, Gautier's revisions to the last stanza, especially his deletion of the earlier "Et chaque voyageur s'incline sur son bord," serve to limit the focus of the poem to the disabled poet. The melancholic landscape becomes internalized in the simile "pleurs furtifs" and in the sip of water. The last illusion of movement and life is dispelled as the verb "coule" is frozen by the substantives "cristal" and "diamant."

[9] It is significant that this first quatrain was the most extensively revised. See Jasinski, *L'España* 170-71 for the original drafts.

[10] See Kastner, 145-46. A similar parodic impulse enlivens much of Musset's poetry, his well-known sonnet "Tristesse" for one.

[11] See Van der Tuin 132-38 for a discussion of Gautier's sense of isolation.

Chapter VI : The Poems of 1842

[1] Gautier helped draft the "Rapport à l'intérieur, au nom de la commission chargée de l'examen des projets de monument à la mémoire de l'empéreur Napoléon." Moreover, he opposed the Invalides as Napoleon's final resting place. See Spoelberch de Lovenjoul 231-36.

[2] By the end of 1842, Gautier had written a total of thirty-nine articles for a variety of newspapers and journals (See *Correspondance* 1, 286, for specific publications).

[3] His evocation transforms floral spectacle into a sinister orgy: "l'aloès ouvre son éventail de lames azurées, l'oranger contourne son bois noueux et s'accroche de ses doigts de racines aux déchirures des escarpements . . . un laurier, d'un bord du chemin à l'autre, va embrasser un cactus, malgré ses épines" (*VE* 234). This dalliance culminates three paragraphs later in the embrace of sun and flowering shrub, the effect being that of an electrifying theatrical pose: "Au moment où je le vis, c'était comme une explosion de fleurs, comme le bouquet d'un feu d'artifice végétal; une fraîcheur splendide et vigoureuse, presque bruyante. . . . Ses belles fleurs jaillissaient avec toute l'ardeur du désir vers la pure lumière du ciel; ses nobles feuilles, taillées tout exprès par la nature pour couronner la gloire, lavées par la bruine des jets d'eau, étincelaient comme des émeraudes au soleil" (*VE* 235-36). There is a tension here between static and dynamic, between the laurel's upward thrust and its lapidary fixedness. Gautier would revisit the subject in *España* ("Le Laurier du Generalife"), but not until a year later.

[4] He adds: "Il ne faudrait pas cependant s'imaginer que les anciennes pièces espagnoles fussent exclusivement sublimes. Le grotesque, cet élément indispensable de l'art au moyen âge, s'y glisse sous la forme du gracioso et du

bobo (niais), qui égaye le sérieux de l'action par des plaisanteries et des jeux de mots plus ou moins hasardés, et produit, à côté du héros, l'effet de ces nains difformes, à pourpoint bariolé, jouant avec des lévriers plus grands qu'eux, qu'on voit figurer auprès de quelque roi ou quelque prince dans les vieux portraits des galeries" (*VE* 291).

[5] By the end of 1841, Gautier had completed the narrative that would become the first part of chapter 11 of *Voyage en Espagne* and which describes the journey from Toledo to the gates of Grenada. The second part of chapter 11, an account of the traveler's experiences in Grenada, was published in 1842 in the July 15 edition of the *Revue des Deux Mondes*. The *feuilleton* that became chapter 12 appeared in *La Revue des Deux Mondes* on August 15, 1842.

[6] Jasinski notes that Gautier was "gêné par une connaissance insuffisante de la langue. Au début du voyage il ne savait que les quelques mots indispensables aux besoins courants; encore le devinait-on souvent plus qu'on ne le comprenait. Après trois mois de séjour il convenait que l'espagnol n'est pas aussi aisé qu'il en a l'air (Jasinski, *L'España* 15).

[7] Spoelberch de Lovenjoul credits Gautier with two other poems in 1842. One is an addition to his earlier "Un Tableau de Valdès Léal" (subsequently entitled "Deux Tableaux de Valdès Léal"), which was published with the *feuilleton* entitled "Andalousie, Cordoue, Séville" (chapters 13 and 14 of *Voyage en Espagne*) in the November 1 edition of *the Revue des Deux Mondes*. One other poem, "A des amis qui partent," appeared towards the end of 1842 but it was not intended for *España*. See Spoelberch de Lovenjoul 248 and 299-300 for the circumstances of its publication. "Sainte Casilde" transposes—and transforms—a painting by Juan Rizi of the martyred saint Centolla. According to Jasinski, Gautier mistakenly attributed it to fra Diego de Leyva, whose painting of the saint nearby does not depict a martyr. The canvas Gautier describes would have been by Juan Rizi and is of Saint Centolla, who unlike Saint Casilde did die a martyr's death (Jasinski, *L'España* 71). Patrick Berthier is of the opinion that Gautier was not mistaken, since he (Gautier) writes of having seen the painting on three separate occasions, naming de Leyva each time (Berthier 587, note 6, 460 of his edition of *Voyage en Espagne*). Gautier's poem describes a fainting figure whose severed breasts lie nearby in a silver basin. An angel bearing a palm frond descends to her. Although an earlier version of the poem exists, there is no way of knowing whether "Sainte Casilde" was written before or after "In Deserto,"

since the two poems were published together. Spoelberch de Lovenjoul assigns it the later number, but gives no reason for doing so. See his interpaged edition of *l'Histoire des Œuvres de Théophile Gautier.*

[8] See page 56.

[9] Jasinski devotes several pages to Gautier's desert, quoting the relevant sections from *Voyage en Espagne* with a view to determining its accuracy ("L'impression était-elle juste?" [Jasinski, *L'España* 143]). He concludes that Gautier "force donc la réalité, et la disproportion éclate surtout dans les vers, où, cédant visiblement au symbole, il resserre et généralise tout à la fois: on a pu voir que malgré la mention *La Guardia,* plusieurs détails se rapportent à l'Andalousie et non plus seulement à la Manche. Qu'on lui rende justice pourtant: s'il a mis en ces paysages trop de désolation tragique, il en a rendu heureusement, tant en prose qu'en vers, la crudité de lignes et la violence des tons" (144). However, Jasinski faults the piece for its "pathétique un peu déclamatoire" (144).

[10] See, for example, Sainte-Beuve, *Reprise* IX "Sonnet" (287-88), XXII "Il y faudrait de la musique de Gluck" (311) and *Refrain*: "Désert du cœur" (Sainte-Beuve 349-50).

[11] Riffaterre assigns to it only the function of the first section, that of establishing aridity (9). In limiting the metaphorical potential of the description (primarily by arguing that there is no *direct* correspondence between vehicle and tenor but only between vehicle and sign), he denies that description the possibilites of extension and indirection that depend upon contradiction, or better, literal unreality. The "lost voice" that he claims is found again— thanks to the hint in the absent "vox clamans" of the title—has coexisted with with the simple appeal for love from the outset because of the "mimesis hurdle" (6). Alan Buisine, among others, objects to such a limited approach, noting that "The greater the condemnation of the practice of mimesis, the more useful it has seemed to learn its functioning. Its excommunication from the realm of fiction has assured its return to the critical scene. . . . It is inconceivable to pass over in silence the imaginary look, retaining only the linguistic and semantic mechanisms of description which function in a closed system, as though description were self-engendering, removed from any act of seeing . . ." (Buisine, 261-63).

[12] It also supports Van der Tuin's contention that "Son (Gautier's) attitude devant la vie est surtout passive" (Van der Tuin 46). Gautier's fascination with the hermaphrodite is apparent in his predilection for combining feminine and

masculine qualities in his poetry and his fiction, notably in *Mademoiselle de Maupin*. According to Raymond Giraud, this "hermaphroditisme esthétique" (the phrase is Van der Tuin's, see 100, note 1), was encouraged by a wave of interest in transvestitism and androgyny, especially in the figure of Shakespeare's Rosalind. With Gautier, it "commands the awareness of an esthetically pleasing disparity, incongruity . . . that communicates in addition something of the thrill of the unknown" (Giraud, "Winckelmann" 8). See Van der Tuin 99-103, Ross Chambers 641-58, and Pierre Albouy 600-608.

[13] Tennant concludes that Gautier "points towards the myth of poetic sterility which was to preoccupy Rimbaud, Mallarmé, and Valéry," citing Théodore in *Mademoiselle de Maupin:* "Leur plus beau poème est celui qu'ils n'ont pas écrit" (*MM* 153-54). Mallarmé's tribute to Gautier in "Toast funèbre" celebrates his poetic silence as a heroic virtue.

[14] Jasinski notes that in the *Residencia de la Santa Caridad* in Seville, which Gautier visited, there was a painting by Murillo of Moses striking the rock (Jasinski, *L'España* 225). The canvas may have helped inspire "In Deserto."

[15] "La vue du Parthénon m'a guéri de ma maladie gothique" [*Souvenirs* 13].

[16] One should not make too much of the religious element in the poems of this year, but it should not be dismissed altogether. The three poems of 1842 in one way or another propose the sinner's progress towards grace as a parallel to the poet's quest, as it were. The three women in "Les Trois Grâces de Grenade" bear names that signify the requisite stages of mystical union with God: martyrdom (Martirio), suffering (Dolores), and grace (Gracia); "In Deserto" and "Sainte Casilde" propose Moses and the angel as intermediaries. Moreover, the alterations in Gautier's transposition of the painting of the martyr in "Sainte Casilde" replicate the biblical figuration of "In Deserto": the poet has added a silver bowl to receive the saint's blood and a palm extended to her by the angel. These images dramatizing her suffering and reward roughly parallel the rod and waters—and possibly the experience—of "In Deserto." "Sainte Casilde" could be said either to recapitulate or prefigure the experience of "In Deserto."

[17] David Scott, in *Pictorialist Poetics*, notes, "The poets of the next generation (Gautier, Banville, Baudelaire) will seek in their poetry to frame or fix the constantly fleeting horizons of Hugolian poetry, and, in doing so, will adopt strophic forms both more compact, foreclosed, and less susceptible to rhetorical subversion than those employed by Hugo" (D. Scott 76). P. E. Tennant notes of *España* that it "shares for the last time the sombre, confessional

rhetoric of *La Comédie de la Mort*, yet foreshadows, particularly in a certain artistic realism allied to a fanciful romance form, the peculiar genre of the forthcoming *Emaux et Camées*" (Tennant 58).

Chapter VII: The Poems of 1843

[1] "L'Enfant de la Montagne" had been written in 1839 and added to the collection.

[2] See chapter 1, note 26. Claude-Marie Senninger writes: "Son esthétique de la prose semble donc en avance, comme l'a bien montré Jasinski, sur son esthétique poétique" (Senninger 54).

[3] C.-A. Fusil remarks of *Emaux et Camées* that "le poète est absent de son œuvre" (Fusil 27).

[4] See Jasinski, *L'España* 81-86, for a discussion of this adaptation. "Mais si la forme du romance ne pouvait être reproduite exactement, l'allure et l'esprit ont été conservés" (83).

[5] Jasinski attributes much of this poem to Gautier's earlier mentors, notably Hugo, Barbier, and Lamartine. He also notes that that a good deal of Villon found its way into the piece, which is not surprising considering that Gautier was revising his *Les Grotesques* at the time that "Les Affres de la mort" was published. See Jasinski, *L'España* 262-68.

[6] In *Voyage en Espagne,* for example, one reads: "Le besoin du vrai, si repoussant qu'il soit, est un trait caractéristique de l'art espagnol: l'idéal et la convention ne sont pas dans le génie de ce peuple, dénué complètement d'esthétique" (*VE* 50). Many critics, including Jasinski, consider Gautier's condemnations rash and uninformed, his perspective warpée: "Il a trop souvent grossi et simplifié." See my page 98, note 3 for a discussion of "Deux tableaux de Valdès Léal."

[7] Claude-Marie Senninger endeavors to show Gautier's progress in *España* towards a Parnassian esthetic through an examination of sources. She maintains that the two quatrains of this sonnet are Parnassien in their use of "épithètes homériques" whereas the two tercets "penchent vers le romantisme" (Senninger 55). According to Jasinski, both the sonnet and the painting were inspired by Aeschylus' *Prometheus Bound* (Jasinski, *L'España* 114-16).

[8] Gautier had at one point considered writing the piece in quatrains. See Jasinski, *L'España* 116.

[9] In fairness to Ribeira, it must be noted that there are no "cascades" in his painting of the subject. Gosselin-Schick observes, " 'Sur le Prométhée du musée de Madrid' effects its detachment from the Spanish artifact in order to faithfully evoke the otherness of that artifact, in order to evoke its absence in the poem's textual (and nymphic) discourse" (99).

[10] Here again Jasinski finds Gautier's judgment skewed by his failure to judge the whole of Montañès' work. "Montañès entre tous, loin de se complaire dans l'horrible, a sculpté pour les confréries pieuses des Christs, des Madones, des moines en prière, où la vérité du détail n'exclut ni la noblesse de l'attitude, ni l'intensité de l'expression; toutes les émotions divines et humaines vivent dans ces œuvres émouvantes . . ." (Jasinski, *L'España* 105). It is also worth noting that in *Voyage en Espagne,* Gautier has nothing good to say of Madrid, which represented to him progress at its most ruinous. His prejudice may have poisoned his appreciations of what he found there.

[11] Fastening upon the "satanic" element in the last four lines of the poem, G. Brunet observes, "Rien n'est plus baudelairien que le poème Madrid et comme sujet et comme frisson et comme technique" (G. Brunet 328).

[12] See Chambers 641-58, for a discussion of Gautier's "complex."

Chapter VIII: The Last Year

[1] Two poems, "Letrilla" and "J'ai laissé sur mon sein de neige," appeared in 1845 and were added to *Poésies complètes*. Gautier also wrote lines 63 to 76 of "Deux Tableaux de Valdès Léal" (originally "Un Tableau de Valdès Léal"), which were added to the 1845 volume.

[2] "Avec quelle furie et quelle volupté / Tu retournes la peau du martyr qu'on écorche, / Pour nous en faire voir l'envers ensanglanté!" (*PC* 2, 274).

[3] According to Jasinski, the poem was inspired by a Breton proverb (Jasinski, *L'España* 255).

[4] Tennant discerns a "universal mobility" in much of Gautier's later poetry: "Matter itself is interchangeable, the apparently static is elusive . . . the senses constantly merge and interact" (Tennant 62-63).

[5] Jasinski maintains that "C'est une romance que Gautier a voulu faire" (Jasinski, *L'España* 205), but he, like many others, uses the term loosely to designate a popular song. The Spanish *romance* describes a ballad of folk origin that developed after the decline of the epic. Romances are generally classified according to their date of composition or to their content. Though the romance varies in length, its meter is octosyllabic, with assonance in the even lines.

The form that Gautier imitates in "J'allais partir . . . ," though basically octosyllabic, is a more complex poetic form, that of the *copla de pie quebrado:* it is described as "a metrical stanza normally comprising six lines of which the 1st, 2nd, 4th, and 5th are octosyllabic, and the 3rd and 6th tetrasyllabic. The rhyme scheme is variable: abcabc; aabaab; aabccb" (*Oxford Companion* 465). See Jasinski, *L'España* 204-5, for the Spanish verses that inspired Gautier. See also Ernest Martinenche's discussion of Gautier's borrowings from Spanish verse forms in his *L'Espagne et le romantisme* 189-92. Finally, given the debt Gautier owed to his Spanish models in these later poems, it is difficult to accept Gosselin-Schick's thesis that Spain is altogether absent from *España*, as she maintains. See Gosselin-Schick 103.

[6] At the same time, "Bobine," which can mean "mug" in the sense of "face," resonates with the lady's name "Balbine," which hints at "babine" or "chops," which is no less vulgar than "mug."

[7] See Jasinski, *L'España* 195 for the Spanish sources of "La Lune."

[8] A more obvious example of synaesthetic effect would be "longs soupirs de feuillages" in "La Fontaine du cimetière," which Gautier wrote in 1841. (Baudelaire had discerned Gautier's "immense intelligence innée de la correspondance et du symbolisme universels" [*BOC*, 2, 689]). Matoré notes that "tandis que Gautier traduit l'idée en termes visuels, quand celle-ci est affectée d'une certaine matérialité, il ne la transpose en termes empruntés au vocabulaire sonore que si elle est imprécise, si 'sous la forme exprimée, on sent une pensée vague, infinie, inexprimable, comme une idée musicale'" (Matoré, *Vocabulaire* 201).

[9] The *vers impair* can be found before the nineteenth century, but rarely. Kastner provides a brief history of it (Kastner 154-58), noting that Ronsard and Voltaire had used it. Jacques Barzun, in *An Essay on French Verse,* notes that in the nineteenth century, the *vers impair* is often used "to prevent 'squareness' " (Barzun 97). He adds that Verlaine was inspired by Hugo's "La Fête chez Thérèse" when he incorporated the *vers impair* into his *Fêtes Galantes* (97).

[10] Fauchereau quotes the musical Gautier at some length here, remarking "Quel Vielé-Griffin, quel Van Lerberghe . . . quel Symboliste enfin n'aurait pas signé ces vers? Et quant aux vers suivants, ils furent publiés douze ans avant la naissance de celui qui recommandait 'de la musique avant toute chose' et l'utilisation du vers impair:

> Regardez les branches,
> Comme elles sont blanches!
> Il neige des fleurs.
> Riant dans la pluie,
> Le soleil essuie
> Les saules en pleurs,
> Et le ciel reflète
> Dans la violette
> Ses pures couleurs.

Qui d'autre écrivait ainsi en 1832?" (Fauchereau 69). Even Jasinski maintains that "C'est par la chanson qu'il [Gautier] inclinera peu à peu vers la forme amenuisée des *Emaux et Camées*" (Jasinski, *L'España* 213). Though critics speak frequently of poetry as music, what is meant precisely by the "musicality" of poetry is not always clear. The relationship of music to poetry has a long and complex history. H. T. Kirby-Smith notes that Eustache Deschamps, in *L'Art de Dictier*, was one of the first to "pry poetry loose from its musical context" (Kirby-Smith 94) and to claim for it its own "musique naturele—rhythm and aural effects belonging to language itself" (97). (J. E. Jackson, in "Baudelaire lecteur de Gautier: Les Deux Horloges," acknowledges the importance of such rhythmical effects to Gautier's lyricism in his discussion of the allegorical *Heures* in Gautier's poem: "Cette picturalisation du temps va de pair, sur le plan du rythme cette fois avec une régularité du vers qu'il est difficile d'interpréter autrement que comme une tentative de maîtriser l'angoisse inhérente à la fuite temporelle par un balancement qui, s'il rappelle un mouvement d'horloge, contribue aussi à en apaiser la violence par l'équilibre de son déroulement" [444].) Of the French Symbolists, Kirby-Smith observes: "It was not so much a case of poetry aspiring to the condition of music as of poetry putting itself to school to learn from music what it ought to aspire to" (Kirby-Smith 272). He contends that it was Valéry who "solved the challenge to the Symbolists of nineteenth-century music, especially Wagner's, by increasing the structured density of poetic sound effects—the *musique naturelle* of Deschamps—beyond that ever achieved in French before and possibly beyond anything ever written in any language" (258-59).

[11] Though the fact is not made much of, Gautier was also a playwright. His trip to Spain inspired a collaborative effort with Paul Siraudin, a vaudeville entitled *Un Voyage en Espagne* (1843). It is the counterpart of *Voyage en Espagne* in

that it parodies much of what is parodied in the travel narrative, especially the mania for local color. But it also champions the popular theater while satirizing its excesses. To that extent it is a measure of Gautier's sympathies with popular taste in theater if not in poetry. For a fuller discussion see Claude Book-Senninger's *Théophile Gautier, auteur dramatique*.

[12] It is worth noting here that the four sonnets of *España* postdate the writing of "In Deserto," and that all of them are divided into hemistiches. Freeman Henry ("Théophile Gautier et l'avenir du sonnet") has demonstrated Gautier's role in defending the exigencies of the Ronsardian sonnet as a musical rather than cerebral form of poetry.

[13] Jasinski adds that there were other factors: "Et puis, les temps héroïques étaient passés; le Romantisme s'embourgeoisait, s'alourdissait de théories politiques et sociales, se défendait mal des imitateurs insincères. Le petit groupe des âmes d'élite, fidèles à l'art et au beau, allait chaque jour diminuant" (Jasinski, *L'España* 271).

[14] "Adieux à la poésie" was not the last of Gautier's poetic efforts to appear before *Emaux et Camées*. There were others that were published in 1845. "Letrilla" and "J'ai laissé sur mon sein de neige" were added to *España* in *Poésies complètes* in 1845. "Prière" and "Gazhel" were added to "Poésies nouvelles" in the same edition of the complete poems. It is possible that Gautier had written them, or had begun work on them, before composing "Adieux à la poésie." In any event, of the four, "Prière" could be considered to follow that poem. In it a "jeune fille, isolée et orpheline," appeals to the Virgin for help and guidance. Jasinski comments, "Nous ne savons malheureusement qui est 'la jeune orpheline'" (*PC* 1, lxvi). It could have been Gautier.

[15] "La letrilla est une composition, le plus souvent étendue, en petits vers. Il y a des letrillas à refrain (*con estribillo*), dans lesquelles une pensée piquante se répète à chaque strophe. Mais toujours le genre est précieux, spirituel, alerte de rythme et de ton" (Jasinski, *L'España* 200). Jasinski notes of Gautier's adaptation: "Le développement est trop court, le vers trop lent, l'expression trop plaintive" (200).

[16] See Spoelberch de Lovenjoul 300-301. These fragments are not dated, but Lovenjoul includes them among the pieces written between June and August of 1845. Lines from "Letrilla" are cited in the Introduction.

[17] Jasinski notes that Gautier wrote only three poems between July of 1845 and January of 1849. See Jasinski, *L'España* 271, note 3.

[18] Jasinski observes, "De 1840 à 1845 Gautier avait senti décroître, avec sa confiance en lui-même, la spontanéité, le jaillissement, et comme la source vive de son talent; sans nul doute, il avait eu de la peine à achever le volume de *Poésies complètes*. Désormais c'en sera fait des longs abandons avec la Muse, des pièces à rythme large où s'épanchait son cœur" (Jasinski, *L'España* 271).

Chapter IX: *España* Revisited

[1] See chapter 1. Early criticism of *España* tended to be both divided and unspecific. Gustave Lanson described *España* as "le vrai commencement du naturalisme" (Lanson 228), whereas Faguet observed, "*España* est presque tout en entier un chef-d'oeuvre." Though he singles out "In Deserto" for special praise, it is Gautier's sense of color and definition that he most appreciates in this and other poems. Baudelaire remarked, "personne, depuis tant d'années, n'a trouvé d'argent ni de loisir pour *Albertus, La Comédie de la Mort* et *Espagna* [sic]. Cela est bien dur à avouer pour un Français, et si je ne parlais pas d'un écrivain placé assez haut pour assister tranquillement à toutes les injustices, j'aurais, je crois, préféré cacher cette infirmité de notre public" (*BOC* 2, 105). The most recent study of Gautier's subjectivity, E. G. Lien's "The Prefatory Poetics of Théophile Gautier," is also devoted in part to *España*. Lien notes of it: "The voyage upon which we embark is at once a geographical displacement and an itinerant exploration of the poet's psyche as seen in the attendant themes of death, violence, love, forgetfulness, and the passing of time. The poet's imagination then transforms his description of the voyage in such a way that the presented exterior world materializes his various states of mind; yet these attitudes must in turn be transformed to fit into the poem's thematic and structural framework. Reality, be it exterior or interior, necessarily undergoes transfiguration in the process of poetic creation" (51). Lien's analysis of the relation of substance to shape in *España*, though brief, is not unlike our own. Finally, it is difficult to accept Gosselin-Schick's conclusion that the volume wanders in search of an absence, when Gautier was so clearly in search of his muse ("Wandering in search of its absence by means of otherness, *España*'s voice is one which strains to be other, and which must do so inadequately, for otherwise, it would make of the other self and/or be present to the self in the other" [Gosselin-Schick 106]).

[2] Burnett observes, "Dans *Emaux et Camées* . . . on ne trouve plus de bâtiments grandioses destinés à contenir un idéal quelconque. L'idéal absolu qui

demandait à être encadré par une forme publique qui reflétait son pouvoir et sa singularité est remplacé par une vision à la fois plus modeste et plus riche. . . . Dans 'Fumée,' une chaumière . . . est un exemple d'une structure modeste qui ne contient pas l'idéal, mais plutôt un être privilégié tout simplement par la poétisation du sujet" (Burnett, "Métaphore" 49).

[3] The term is Houston's: "His cinematic technique produces a faceting effect, an intricate network of Mallarméan 'reflets réciproques,' the sense of an experience or figure or object being turned through different angles and thus accumulating to itself a variety of images, responses, associations" (Houston 48).

[4] See also Länger 15, 33-34 for a discussion of esthetic emotion.

[5] Claude-Marie Senninger 51.

[6] In fact, his was almost a missionary's zeal: "Pour notre compte, nous aimons assez l'art hiéroglyphique escarpé, où l'on n'entre pas comme chez soi; il faut relever la foule jusqu'à l'œuvre, et non rabaisser l'œuvre jusqu'à la foule" (article written in 1839 and republished in 1858 in *l'Histoire de l'art dramatique en France depuis vingt-cinq ans,* 1). Thomas Bremer, in his "Théophile Gautier: 'Dans la Sierra,' " contends that though Gautier's esthetic may have appeared increasingly elitist, his Spanish experience at least "hat gezeigt, das es keineswegs darum geht, 'die Menge' von den literarischen Erfahrungen insgesamt ausschliessen" (103).

[7] See Jean Starobinski's "Portrait de l'artiste en saltimbanque" for a discussion of the subject.

[8] These efforts reveal a kind of latter-day Rabelais who was often given to writing coarse and obscene doggerel as well as to satirizing the sacrosanct. Fauchereau quotes the following lines, for example:
> Que les chiens sont heureux!
> Dans leur humeur badine
> Ils se sucent la pine,
> Ils s'enculent entre eux;
> Que les chiens sont heureux! (96)

[9] "Shakespeare aux Funambules" (*Souvenirs d'art et de critique* 56). This article was originally published in the *Revue de Paris*, 4 September 1842.

[10] G. Brunet observes "Gautier a vu clairement que le salut pour lui était dans la concentration. Il a vu qu'un artiste du détail, qui perçoit séparément le monde physique et le monde moral devait renoncer aux longs développements, aux grand lieux communs, aux thèmes gonflés d'infini . . ." (G. Brunet 323).

[11] He adds, "Spirite a été écrit, en partie, pour dissiper un malentendu: Gautier voulait redresser son image aux yeux de la postérité. Et il paraît déjà répondre aux critiques à venir lorsqu'il prend des attitudes apparemment plus conformes aux impératifs du sentiment et à la religion de l'ineffable" (Tortonese 80). William Allen, in his review of Freeman Henry's *Relire Théophile Gautier: le plaisir du texte*, observes "Since the centenary of Gautier's death in 1972, critical interest in the writer has effectively served to redeem his reputation" (Allen 370).

Bibliography

Works by Théophile Gautier

Caprices et Zigzags. Paris: Hachette, 1856.
Correspondance générale. Genève-Paris: Librairie Droz, 2 vols., 1985.
"Du Beau dans l'art." *Revue des Deux Mondes*. 1 July 1847: 887-908.
Histoire de l'art dramatique en France depuis vingt-cinq ans. 1858. Geneva: Slatkine Reprints, 1968.
Histoire du romantisme. Paris: Charpentier, 1911.
Les Jeunes-France, romans goguenards...suivis de contes humoristiques. Paris: Charpentier, 1873.
Mademoiselle de Maupin. Ed. A. Boschot, Paris: Garnier, 1966.
Poésies (1830). Ed. Harry Cockerham, London: Athlone Press, 1973.
Poésies complètes. Ed. René Jasinski, 3 vols. Paris: Nizet, 1970.
Portraits contemporains. Paris: Charpentier, 1898.
Quand on Voyage. Paris: Michel-Lévy, 1865.
"Shakespeare aux Funambules." *Souvenirs d'art et de critique*. Paris: Charpentier, 1883.
Voyage en Espagne. Paris: Charpentier, 1879.
Voyage en Espagne et España. Ed. Patrick Berthier. Paris: Gallimard, 1981.

Other works

Albouy, Pierre. "Le Mythe de l'Androgyne dans *Mademoiselle de Maupin*." *Revue d'Histoire Littéraire de la France* (July-August 1972): 600-608.
Allen, William. Rev. of *Relire Théophile Gautier: le plaisir du texte,* Freeman Henry, ed. *French Review* 74, (December 2000) 2, 370-71.

Avallone-Le Tourneau, Cécile. "La théâtralité de la mort dans les premières poésies de Théophile Gautier." *Bulletin de la Société Théophile Gautier*, 18 (1996): 109-23.

Bailbé, Joseph-Marc. "L'Expression de la mort dans *España*." *Bulletin de la Société Théophile Gautier*, 18 (1996): 125-34.

Barbey d'Aurevilly, Jules-Amédée. *Le XIXe siècle: Les Œuvres et les Hommes.* 2 vols. Paris: Mercure de France, 1964.

Barzun, Jacques. *An Essay on French Verse.* New York: New Directions, 1991.

Baudelaire, Charles. *Œuvres Complètes.* 2 vols. Paris: Gallimard, 1976.

Benesch, Rita. *Le Regard de Théophile Gautier.* Zurich: Schaffhouse und Bibern, 1969.

Bergerat, Emile. *Théophile Gautier: entretiens, souvenirs et correspondance.* Paris: Charpentier, 1911.

Berthier, Patrick. "Préface" to *Voyage en Espagne, suivi d'España* by Théophile Gautier. Paris: Gallimard, 1981.

Book-Senninger, Claude. *Théophile Gautier, auteur dramatique.* Paris: Nizet, 1972.

Boschot, Adolphe. *Théophile Gautier.* Paris: Desclée de Brouwer, 1933.

Bremer, Thomas. "Théophile Gautier: Dans la Sierra." *Die Französchen Lyrik des 19. Jahrhunderts.* Munich: Fink, 1987, 93-109.

Brunet, François. "A propos d'un vers de 'L'Escurial.' " *Bulletin de la Société Théophile Gautier* (2000), 187-96.

Brunet, Gabriel. "Théophile Gautier, poète." *Mercure de France* (1922), 289-332.

Brunetière, Ferdinand. *L'Evolution de la poésie lyrique en France au dix-neuvième siècle.* Paris: Hachette, 1894.

Brunot, Ferdinand, Daniel Mornay, and Paul Hazard. *Le Romantisme et les lettres.* Paris: Aubier, 1929.

Buisine, Alain. "The First Eye." *Towards a Theory of Description. Yale French Studies*: 61 (1981), 261-75.

Bulgin, Kathleen. *The Making of an Artist: Gautier's 'Voyage en Espagne.'* Birmingham: Summa, 1988.

Burnett, David. "The Architecture of Meaning: Gautier and Romantic Architectural Visions." *French Forum:* 2 (1982), 109-16.

———. "Métaphore et signification architecturales dans les poésies de Théophile Gautier." *Bulletin de la Société Théophile Gautier* 5 (1983): 41-52.

———. "Sur la Composition de La Comédie de la mort." *Bulletin de la Société Théophile Gautier* 2 (1980): 1-8.

Butor, Michel. "Le Voyage et l'écriture." *Romantisme* 4 (1972), 11-17.

Cellier, Léon. "Présentation." *Revue d'Histoire Littéraire de la France* 72 [July-August 1972], 577-82).

———. "Gautier, un écrivain d'avenir." *Nouvelles Littéraires*, November 1972: 4.

Chambers, Ross. "Gautier et le complexe de Pygmalion." *Revue d'Histoire Littéraire de la France* 72 (July-August 1972): 641-58.

Court-Perez, Francine. *Gautier, un romantique ironique.* Paris: Honoré Champion, 1998.

Crouzet, Michel. "Gautier et le problème de 'créer.' " *Revue d'Histoire Littéraire de la France* 72 (July-August 1972), 659-87.

Delvaille, Bernard. *Théophile Gautier.* Paris: Seghers, 1968.

Dillingham, Louise. *The Creative Imagination of Théophile Gautier.* Princeton: Psychological Monographs, Psychological Review Co., 1927.

Dineen, R. M. "The Poetry of Théophile Gautier: A Search for Utopia." Journal of the Australasian Universities Modern Language Association 41 (1974): 50-63.

Du Camp, Maxime. *Théophile Gautier.* Paris: Hachette, 1890.

Faguet, Emile. "De l'influence de Théophile Gautier." *Revue des Deux Mondes* 4 (1911): 327-41.

———. *Le XIXe siècle des œuvres et des hommes: études littéraires.* Paris: Boivin et Cie., 1887.

Fauchereau, Serge. *Théophile Gautier.* Paris: Denoël, 1972.

Fernandez Sanchez, C. "Gautier en Espagne." *Bulletin de la Socété Théophile Gautier,* 5 (1983), 155-57.

Feydeau, Ernest. *Souvenirs intimes.* Paris: Plon, 1874.

Fontainas, A. "Les Poésies de Théophile Gautier." *Mercure de France* 16 September 1911.

Friedrich, Hugo. *The Structure of Modern French Poetry.* Northwestern University Press: Evanston, 1974.

Fusil, C.-A. *Théophile Gautier, Pages Choisies.* N.d. Classiques Larousse.

Fussell, Paul. *Abroad: British Literary Traveling between the Wars.* New York: Oxford University Press, 1980.

Gide, André. *Incidences.* Paris: Gallimard, 1924.

Giraud, Raymond. "Gautier's Dehumanization of Art." *L'Esprit Créateur* 3 (1963): 3-9.

———. "Winckelmann's Part in Gautier's Perception of Classical Beauty." *Yale French Studies* 38 (1967): 172-82.

Goncourt, Edmond and Jules Goncourt. *Journal des Goncourt*, 4 vols. Paris: Charpentier, 1887.

Gosselin-Schick, Constance. *Seductive Resistance: The Poetry of Théophile Gautier.* Amsterdam/Atlanta: Rodopi, 1994.

Harvey, Paul and J. E. Heseltine. *The Oxford Companion to French Literature.* Oxford: Clarendon Press, 1961.

Henry, Freeman. "Relire Théophile Gautier." *Relire Théophile Gautier. Le plaisir du texte*, ed. Freeman Henry. Amsterdam / Atlanta: Rodopi, 1998, 1-10.

———. "Théophile Gautier et l'avenir du sonnet." *Bulletin de la Société Théophile Gautier* 21 (1999): 95-103.

Houssaye, Arsène. *Les Confessions. Souvenirs d'un demi-siècle littéraire.* 6 vols. Paris: E. Dentu, 1888-91.

Houston, John Porter. *French Symbolism and the Modernist Movement.* Baton Rouge and London: Louisiana State University Press, 1980.

Jackson, J. E. "Baudelaire lecteur de Gautier: Les Deux Horloges." *Revue d'Histoire Littéraire de la France*, 1984, 439-49.

Jasinski, René. *Les Années romantiques de Théophile Gautier.* Paris: Vuibert, 1929.

———. *L''España' de Théophile Gautier.* Paris: Vuibert, 1929.

Kastner, L. E. *A History of French Versification.* Oxford: Clarendon Press, 1903.

Kermode, Frank. *An Appetite for Poetry.* Cambridge, Massachusetts: Harvard University Press, 1989.

Kirby-Smith, H. T. *The Celestial Twins: Poetry and Music through the Ages.* Amherst: University of Massachusetts Press, 1999.

Länger, Suzanne. *Feeling and Form.* New York: Scribner, 1953.

Lanson, Gustave. *Histoire de la littérature française.* Paris: Hachette, 1894.

Levey, Michael. Rev. of *Théophile Gautier: A Romantic Critic of the Visual Arts,* by Robert Snell (Oxford UP, 1982), in *The Burlington Magazine* 125 (July 1983): 434-35.

Lewis, Roy. *On Reading French Verse.* Oxford: Clarendon Press, 1982.

Lien, E. G. "The Prefatory Poetics of Théophile Gautier." *Romance Notes* 32 (1991), 47-54.
Lipschutz, Ilse. *Spanish Painting and the French Romantics*. Cambridge, Massachusetts: Harvard University Press, 1972.
Little, Roger. *The Shaping of Modern French Poetry: Reflections on Unrhymed Poetic Form, 1840-1990*. Manchester: Carcanet Press; Paris: Alyscamps Press, 1995.
Martin, Graham Dunstan. *Language, Truth and Poetry*. Edinburgh: Edinburgh University Press, 1975.
Martinenche, Ernest. *L'Espagne et le romantisme*. Paris: Hachette, 1922.
Martino, Pierre. *Parnasse et symbolisme*. Paris: Colin, 1925.
Matoré, George. *La Préface de Mademoiselle de Maupin*. Ed. critiqué par Georges Matoré. Paris: Droz, 1946.
———. *Le Vocabulaire et la société sous Louis-Phillippe*. Paris: Droz, 1951; Geneva: Slatkine Reprints, 1967.
Michaud, G. F. *Mallarmé*. Paris: Hatier-Boivin, 1953.
Nerval, Gérard de. *Journey to the Orient*. New York: New York Univ. Press, 1972.
Porter, Laurence M. *The Crisis of French Symbolism*. Ithaca and London: Cornell University Press, 1990.
Poulet, Georges. *Trois essais de mythologie romantique*. Paris: Corti, 1966.
———. *La Pensée Indéterminée, II, Du Romantisme au XX siècle*. Paris: PUF, 1987.
Reybaud, Louis. *Jerome Paturot a la recherche d'une position sociale*. Paris: Michel Lévy Frères, 1842.
Richardson, Joanna. *Théophile Gautier*. New York: Coward-McCann, 1959.
Riffaterre, Michael. *Semiotics and Poetry*. Bloomington: Indiana U.P., 1968.
Sainte-Beuve, C.-A. *Poésies complètes*. Paris: Alphonse Lemerre, 1879.
Scott, Clive. *A Question of Syllables: Essays in Nineteenth-Century French Verse*. New York: Cambridge University Press, 1986.
Scott, David. *Pictorialist Poetics: Poetry and the Visual Arts in Nineteenth-Century France*. Cambridge: Cambridge University Press, 1988.
Senninger, Claude-Marie. "*España* à mi-chemin entre *La Comédie de la mort* et *Emaux et Camées*." *Bulletin de la Société Théophile Gautier* 2 (1980): 51-60.
Spoelberch de Lovenjoul, Charles. *Histoire des œuvres de Théophile Gautier*. 2 vols. Paris: Charpentier, 1887. See also Collection Louvenjoul, Chantilly.
Spencer, Michael. *The Art Criticism of Théophile Gautier*. Geneva: Droz, 1969.

Starkie, Enid. *From Gautier to Eliot.* London: Hutchinson, 1960.
Starobinski, Jean. *Portrait de l'artiste en saltimbanque.* Geneva: Skira, 1970.
Tennant, P. E. *Théophile Gautier.* London: Athlone Press, 1975.
Thibaudet, A. *La Poésie de Stéphane Mallarmé.* Paris: La Nouvelle Revue Française, 1926.
Töppfer, R. "Du Beau dans l'art" in *Revue des Deux Mondes.* Paris, 1 July 1847.
Tortonese, Paolo. "L'Echec de Gautier: Hommage à Georges Poulet." *De Baudelaire à Lorca.* 3 vols. Kassel: Reichenberger, 1996, (73-81).
Van der Tuin, Henri. *L'Evolution psychologique, esthétique et littéraire de Théophile Gautier.* Paris: Nizet, 1933.
Ward, Philip. *The Oxford Companion to Spanish Literature.* Oxford: Clarendon Press, 1978.
Whyte, Peter. "Sur le chemin du beau idéal: berceau de l'esthétique gautiériste." *Bulletin de la Société Théophile Gautier* 12 (1990), 441-48.
Williams, Margaret. "Spain as Seen by French Writers between 1825 and 1850." Diss. University of London, 1959.
Winters, Yvor. *Forms of Discovery.* Alan Swallow, 1967.
Zola, Emile. *Le Messager de l'Europe.* July 1879.

Index

Albertus, 13, 15-17, 17n., 18, 24, 25n., 28, 34, 41, 47n., 49, 67, 78, 83n., 85

Balzac, 13, 24
Banville, 13, 62n.
Barbey d'Aurevilly, 5
Baudelaire, 3, 5-7, 13, 14n., 48, 61, 62n., 68-69, 78n., 83n.
Berlioz, 14, 78
Byron, 14, 19n.

Chateaubriand, 26, 27n.
Comédie de la mort, La, 13, 17-19, 19n., 24, 27n., 32-33, 37, 47, 49, 62n.

Deschamps, 78n.
Dante, 17
Dumas, 26

Eliot, 6
Emaux et Camées, 2-3, 5-7, 9, 13, 15, 20, 32-36, 62, 62n., 66n., 71, 78n., 79, 80n., 81, 83n., 84-85

Flaubert, 27

Gide, 6
Goethe, 14
Goncourt, Jules, 36n.

Goya, 25n., 38, 38n., 66
Grotesques, Les, 24, 67n., 85

Heine, 14
Hoffmann, 19n.
Hugo, 11-12, 12n., 13-14, 17n., 28, 32, 34, 43, 47, 48n., 61, 62n., 67n., 68n., 76, 81

Jeunes-France, Les, 24

Lamartine, 12, 17n., 27n., 67n.
Leconte de Lisle, 13
Lope de Vega, 56, 56n.

Mademoiselle de Maupin, 12n., 17, 24, 27n., 28, 35, 60n., 85
Mallarmé, 9n., 53, 59-60, 60n., 84n.
Mérimée, 26
Montesquieu, 23
Moore, 6
Murillo, 61n.
Musset, 14, 17n., 34, 48n., 53n.

Nerval, 13, 27, 27n.

Pater, 6
Pound, 6

Rabelais, 85n.
Ribeira, 47n., 67-68, 68n.

Rimbaud, 60n.
Ronsard, 78n., 80n.

Sand, 12
Sainte-Beuve, 2n., 5-6, 6n., 12, 14, 14n., 48n., 57, 57n.
Shakespeare, 56, 60n., 86n.
Stendhal, 13
Swinburne, 5
Symbolist(s), 3, 9, 34, 78, 78n.
Symons, 6

Valdès, Léal, 31n., 47, 47n., 57, 67, 67n., 73, 73n.
Valéry, 7n., 60n., 78n.
Verlaine, 78, 78n.
Vigny, 12, 17n., 34
Voltaire, 23, 78n.
Voyage en Espagne, Un, 78n.
Voyage en Espagne, 2, 23, 23n., 25, 27-28, 28n., 29-30, 33, 37, 38n., 39-41, 43, 45, 46n., 48n., 55-56, 56n., 57, 57n., 63-67, 67n., 68n., 78n., 85
Villon, 67n.

Wilde, 6
Winters, 7n.

Zola, 6

OHIO UNIVERSITY LIBRARY
Please return this book as soon as you have finished with it. In order to avoid a fine it must